'Daniel's story is very readable and interspersed with really helpful tips and information. The way the ADHD criteria and the strategies the author has found helpful are related directly to the child we are reading about makes them all the easier to understand and the regulations around school exclusions and special needs provision are introduced easily into the narrative too. The book also includes an excellent selection of references and resources. This is a really worthwhile project and I will be recommending it to parents who contact us.'

– Mary Austin, Founder,
ADHD Oxfordshire

'*The Boy from Hell* is like a parents' survival guide, offering private comfort and reassurance that it won't always be like this, and thouendorsementgh every battle may take you to the brink of exhaustion it will all be worth it in the end. Oh, and it's proof that a mother's instinct about her beautiful yet challenging son is always right!'

– Annemarie Main,
mother of a child with ADHD

D0219667

THE BOY
FROM
HELL

of related interest

Specific Learning Difficulties
What Teachers Need to Know
Diana Hudson
Illustrated by Jon English
ISBN 978 1 84905 590 1
eISBN 978 1 78450 046 7

Beating Boredom as the Secret to Managing ADHD
The Elephant in the ADHD Room
Letitia Sweitzer
ISBN 978 1 84905 965 7
eISBN 978 0 85700 910 4

Kids in the Syndrome Mix of ADHD, LD, Autism
Spectrum, Tourette's, Anxiety, and More!
The one-stop guide for parents, teachers,
and other professionals
Martin L. Kutscher, MD
With contributions from Tony Attwood, PhD
and Robert R. Wolff, MD
ISBN 978 1 84905 967 1
eISBN 978 0 85700 882 4

Can I tell you about ADHD?
A guide for friends, family and professionals
Susan Yarney
Illustrated by Chris Martin
Part of the Can I tell you about…? series
ISBN 978 1 84905 359 4
eISBN 978 0 85700 708 7

AD/HD Homework Challenges Transformed!
Creative Ways to Achieve Focus and Attention
by Building on AD/HD Traits
Harriet Hope Green
ISBN 978 1 84905 880 3
eISBN 978 0 85700 601 1

THE BOY FROM HELL

Life with a Child with ADHD

Alison M. Thompson

Foreword by Rory Bremner

Jessica Kingsley *Publishers*
London and Philadelphia

This edition published in 2016
by Jessica Kingsley Publishers
73 Collier Street
London N1 9BE, UK
and
400 Market Street, Suite 400
Philadelphia, PA 19106, USA

www.jkp.com

First published in 2013 by Proof Fairy Publishing

Library of Congress Cataloging in Publication Data
Names: Thompson, Alison M. (Alison Mary), 1971-
Title: The boy from hell : life with a child with
ADHD / Alison M. Thompson ;
    foreword by Rory Bremner.
Description: London : Jessica Kingsley Publishers, 2016. | "First published
    in 2013 by Proof Fairy Publishing"--Title page verso. | Includes
    bibliographical references.
Identifiers: LCCN 2015038779 | ISBN 9781785920158 (alkaline paper)
Subjects: LCSH: Thompson, Alison M. (Alison Mary), 1971---Family. |
    Hyperactive children--England--Biography. | Hyperactive children--Family
    relationships--England. | Mothers and sons--England--Biography. |
    Attention-deficit hyperactivity disorder--Case studies. | Adjustment
    (Psychology)--Case studies.
Classification: LCC RJ506.H9 T46 2016 | DDC 618.92/85890092-
-dc23 LC record available at http://lccn.loc.gov/2015038779

British Library Cataloguing in Publication Data
A CIP catalogue record for this book is available from the British Library

ISBN 978 1 78592 015 8
eISBN 978 1 78450 257 7

Printed and bound in the United States

To Ian, for our children

Disclaimer

Although the author has made every effort to ensure that the information in this book was correct at press time, the author does not assume and hereby disclaims any liability to any party for any loss, damage, or disruption caused by errors or omissions, whether such errors or omissions result from negligence, accident, or any other cause.

This book is not intended as a substitute for the medical advice of physicians. The reader should regularly consult a physician in matters relating to his/her health and particularly with respect to any symptoms that may require diagnosis or medical attention.

Contents

Foreword

I call it my best friend and my worst enemy. The mental condition that allows me to make lateral connections and leaps of imagination, yet leaves me incapable of simple tasks and basic organisation. Even while writing this piece, my mind is flying off in all directions, my concentration wavering, my focus drifting. Yours may be too. Welcome to our world!

Imagine you're a child, being told to sit still, be quiet, pay attention, organise yourself and stay focused. Hard enough. But if you have ADHD – Attention Deficit Hyperactivity Disorder – it's well-nigh impossible. And so the cycle begins: being restless and distracted, getting told off, becoming frustrated and anxious, being excluded from class, feeling stupid and worthless and misunderstood. Imagine the effect that has on a young person; your confidence and self-esteem worn away and broken down by months and years of conflict, frustration and social exclusion, with apparently only yourself to blame. And, ADHD being what it is, almost half of those affected will also struggle with another learning difficulty: Dyslexia, Dyspraxia, even Asperger's Syndrome.

For some, this is too much to bear: 1 in 5 young people with ADHD will attempt suicide by the age of 18. And for the families too, life can become unbearable – a daily battle simply to get through without being driven to tears of frustration and despair.

But you're not alone. It's estimated that 1 child in 20 has ADHD. Let's think about that: it means roughly one child in every classroom – around 500,000 children in the UK alone.

The irony is that these children are often the brightest, the most creative, the most intuitive and intelligent people. They grow up to be actors, comedians and performers like Emma Watson, will.i.am, Robbie Williams and Jim Carrey. Or indeed great sportsmen like Lewis Hamilton, Michael Phelps or Louis Smith.

It's just that there is so much going on in these young brains that their enthusiasm, their restlessness, their hyperactivity is not easily controlled. The condition should really be called attention *surfeit*, not attention deficit.

But there is hope. This book shows that, with (sometimes superhuman!) patience, understanding and management, the condition can be tempered – even overcome.

Alison's story is both heart-breaking and inspiring: her diary entries record in painful detail the desperate experience of living with a child with ADHD. But it has a happy ending. Her ugly duckling has become a swan.

Her account will make you cry. But it may also make you laugh. Above all, it should make you realise that you're not alone. With patience, understanding, professional help and perseverance, you can get through this, and life can get better.

Good luck!

Rory Bremner

Acknowledgements

Many people have played a part in our ADHD journey and I would hate to attempt to name them all for fear of missing someone – so I shall keep this short.

Thanks to everyone who has helped Daniel throughout his life, but special thanks must go to Mrs Brind, Mr Wells, Miss Sheppard, Andrew Paterson, Rachel, Tripz and Debbie.

Thanks to all my friends, who put up with me rambling on about this book for months when I first wrote it. Special thanks to the following people:

My best friend Andrea for putting her life at risk to look after Daniel for me all those years ago

Mark and Sarah for being there when I needed them

My family – but especially my mum for her unending love and support

Steve for filling in the missing piece of our family so well

And Katie and Dan – for without them I would be nothing.

Preface

As a proofreader, I spend much of my time editing manuscripts by aspiring authors. For many years, every time a new manuscript arrived in my inbox I'd find myself wondering why I hadn't written a book yet – it had always been one of those things I wanted to do, and would do…one day. Eventually, I made the decision to get on and do it, and after a writing retreat in Brighton, a few busy weekends at home, months of inactivity and a nudge from a friend, the first edition of *The Boy from Hell: Life with a Child with ADHD* arrived in the world. Little did I know when I self-published the book back in April 2013 that my story would touch the lives of hundreds of families around the country – families who were also living with the challenge of ADHD. The book sold well and was a bronze medal winner in the 2015 Wishing Shelf Independent Book Awards; it was featured in national magazines and was the springboard for me starting a new career helping parents and carers.

I'm delighted that Jessica Kingsley Publishers have decided to publish this, the fully updated second edition of the book. I hope many more parents will identify with our story and feel empowered to support their children to achieve great things.

Alison M. Thompson
September 2015

Introduction

Friday 3rd November 2006: Daniel's a funny little soul. Having ADHD, he can come across as bolshy, in your face, aggressive, over-confident, energetic and brash, but those who know him well know he is also kind, loving, funny, tender, empathetic, caring and very charming. There's also another side to him too, his autistic side, and that makes him inflexible, insecure and shy – and very much a man of routine.

Looking back, I think I knew there was always something different about Daniel. Even as a baby, he was irritable, moody and inflexible. Where his sister had been content, he was angry; where she slipped easily into a routine, he was unpredictable. At the time I put it down to him being a boy, or a second child, or because I didn't have so much time to spend with him.

So when he was diagnosed with Attention Deficit Hyperactivity Disorder at the age of six, it wasn't really a surprise, but I had no idea what the following 12 years would bring – including battles with schools, two permanent exclusions, an educational tribunal, brushes with the law and the emotional journey that ended with a Statement of Educational Needs and a place in special school.

ADHD has been around forever – the first written record of it dates back to 1755[1] – but it's been diagnosed more frequently in the last 30 years and it often gets a bad press. In fact, many people would have you believe it's a made-up condition, an excuse for a lack of parenting skills. But any parent of a child with ADHD knows it's a real, genuine disability that affects every single aspect of a child's life – and the lives of their friends and family too.

So why am I writing this book? As the parent of a young man with ADHD, I read pretty much everything I could find in a bid to find some answers, some strategies that would make our lives better and give Daniel the chance of a productive, safe and happy future. Many of the books out there are authored by medical professionals and most of them are American, so even when I did find something written from the parent's perspective, it wasn't relevant, as the condition is treated very differently in America. For example, ADHD is more readily diagnosed over there, with medication often the first option, whereas in the UK diagnosis can be hard to get and medication a last resort.

What I needed was a book that outlined a UK mother's experience of ADHD along with tips and advice on how to cope with the demands it places on a family.

And when I couldn't find anything that fitted the bill, I decided to write it myself.

I kept a diary for many years and those diary entries were indispensable when I was writing this book. One phrase that kept cropping up throughout the diary was 'the boy from hell' – because at his very worst, Daniel was truly hellish. The strange thing is, although I never actually referred to Daniel as the boy from hell anywhere other than in my private diary, his online nickname now is Hell Boy!

What you'll find in this book is our personal experience of ADHD through schooling, medical intervention, the exclusion process and family life. Our case is unique, as is every family with a child with special needs, but I've included some advice on what I've found helpful along the way, and I hope it will be helpful for other families too. If you have, or suspect you have, a child with ADHD, I hope that reading about our experience will show you that you're not alone and that there is help available – although I can guarantee you'll have to fight for it tooth and nail. Above all else, I wanted to show that ADHD is real, it does exist and it can have serious consequences for everyone involved – but there is also a lot of positivity, love and hope for those affected too.

About ADHD

Attention Deficit Hyperactivity Disorder – otherwise known as ADHD – is a biological condition where the parts of the brain that manage memory, focus, impulsiveness and concentration are affected, leading to children and adults with the condition having a lack of control in those areas.

ADHD affects between 3 and 7 per cent of school-age children, and while the exact cause is not known, evidence points to it being a genetic, hereditary condition. In fact, research has found that in families where one child has been diagnosed with ADHD, there is a 30–40 per cent chance that another sibling will also have the condition; if the siblings are identical twins, the chance increases to 90 per cent.[2]

There are two sets of criteria used to diagnose ADHD: DSM-5 and ICD-10. Although ICD-10 is used across Europe, doctors in the UK tend to use DSM-5 more frequently. It identifies three distinct types of

ADHD: ADHD, Predominantly Hyperactive; ADHD, Predominantly Inattentive; and ADHD, Combined. Kids with ADHD are likely to have short attention spans, be easily distracted and act without thinking. They can be disorganised and forgetful, or fidgety and unable to settle easily. They can also be aggressive, obstructive and rude. ICD-10, which calls the condition Hyperkinetic Disorder, lists similar symptoms, but a child has to be both hyperactive and inattentive to be given a diagnosis. You can find out more about the diagnostic criteria used for DSM-5 and ICD-10 in Appendix 1.

Although some children with ADHD are textbook cases, there are often other symptoms too, related to other disorders such as autism, OCD (Obsessive Compulsive Disorder), ODD (Oppositional Defiant Disorder), Conduct Disorder, Dyslexia, Dyspraxia, anxiety or depression. Because of these additional co-morbidities, no two children with ADHD will show exactly the same symptoms – which, I guess, is why it can be difficult to diagnose.

According to the Office for National Statistics, around 1.7 per cent of the UK population has ADHD. It affects boys more than girls, on a 4 to 1 ratio, and although some children 'grow out' of it – or more likely, learn techniques to deal with it – around 15 per cent of adults diagnosed with ADHD in childhood still have the full range of symptoms and 65 per cent find it affects their daily lives in some way.[3]

Furthermore, a survey[4] of child psychologists, psychiatrists and paediatricians who work in the field of ADHD found that:

- 98 per cent of those surveyed believed undiagnosed ADHD has a serious impact on a child's academic progress.

- Over 90 per cent said that undiagnosed and untreated ADHD:

  - has a serious impact on a child's relationships with their parents, siblings and peers

  - can result in children feeling excluded from their peers, impacting on their ability to make friends and leading to very low self-esteem due to their exclusion

  - can lead to a variety of social problems, such as difficulties finding and keeping a job and criminal behaviour (such as stealing, shoplifting and vandalism).

- 85 per cent said they believe not treating childhood ADHD could lead to adult mental health problems such as depression and even suicide.

With so much evidence to hand, it shocks me that some people – and the media especially – still seem to believe that ADHD is just a label for badly behaved kids. It's a biological condition – a deficiency in the brain – and no child can help whether they have it or not, just as a child with asthma or epilepsy has no choice in their diagnosis.

Even with a diagnosis and proper treatment, children with ADHD have a tough time in life. Forty per cent of all children with ADHD have been excluded from school for a fixed term and 11 per cent have experienced a permanent exclusion.[5]

More worryingly, international research has found that two-thirds of all young men in Young Offender institutions have a history of childhood ADHD, and 50 per cent of men in adult prisons had ADHD as children too.[6]

When I first read that statistic, a shudder went through me – for I know from my own experience with Daniel that at times all I could see for him was a life of violence.

The Early Years

Saturday 14th August 2001: Today has been a horrible, hateful day. Daniel has pushed me to my absolute wits' end. Sometimes it really does feel like he is the original child from hell.

I guess the first real signs that there was something 'wrong' with Daniel showed when he was a toddler. He was always on the go, with more energy than he knew what to do with. At home he wanted constant attention and seemed unable to play on his own. Toys seemed to disintegrate upon his touch – we often called him Demolition Dan – and he was noisy, destructive and naughty.

Some days it seemed like life was an endless torrent of disobedience, backchat, rudeness, name-calling and aggression, all aimed at me. I always liked to praise Daniel's good behaviour but sometimes there was little to praise, and punishments – being sent to his room, being ignored, treats withheld and the very occasional smack – seemed to make no difference.

Trips out were stressful too, because unless I had a firm hold on Daniel he'd be off exploring the world as soon as my back was turned. We started going to the mums and toddlers group at my daughter's school, where Daniel managed to make a few friends, but he spent most mornings rampaging around the room, knocking over the other children's Lego models, causing mayhem and generally being disruptive. Every session ended with story time, and while all the other children settled down on the carpet with their parents or carers, I'd be trying desperately to get Daniel to sit down as he was too busy wanting to run around.

All kids go through the toddler tantrum stage but his seemed more extreme than most. He would scream and shout for hours if he couldn't get his way, if he was tired, if he was frustrated. He would lash out at anyone and anything that got in his way – and woe betide any child who tried to take a toy off him.

As a mother, it was difficult to see my lovely baby turn into this red-faced angry monster and at times I found it difficult to cope. I was never a fan of smacking and I would deal with tantrums by ignoring Daniel if possible, or removing him from the situation if other children were in danger. My action normally resulted in me being whacked or kicked and my arms and legs were constantly covered in bruises from such attacks. Just occasionally, though, I'd snap and hit back – and instantly regret it as the torrent of punches coming my way increased.

I survived by telling myself it was just a stage and he would grow out of it, surely. After all, when he wasn't being so angry and destructive Daniel was a funny, charming, kind and caring child, and the apple of my eye. When he wasn't being the boy from hell, we had a great time together. He was completely fearless; he loved water so much he taught himself to swim at the age of three so he didn't have to go around with me at the swimming pool. He loved being outdoors too, and didn't seem to notice what the weather was doing. I remember one morning when the toddler group had been collecting mini-beasts and leaves in the school grounds. It started raining and all the other mums and toddlers went indoors, but not us – oh no, Daniel was intent on finding a spider and we both got soaked so he could pursue his goal! Other times he quickly tired of things. On a trip to a farm he flitted from one thing to another like a butterfly. 'Sheep. Seen it now. Oh look, cow. Seen it. Can we go in the park now? Goat. Let's go, Mum. Pig. Another pig. Mummy, pleeeeeeeese can I go on the slide now?'

From an early age – and despite his own poor behaviour – Daniel has always had a strong sense of right and wrong, of justice and fairness. On that same farm trip Daniel and his friend were playing in the sandpit when some bigger boys came along and started kicking the sand around. I politely asked them to stop and Daniel, age three, struck his most macho pose and said, 'Yes, don't do that to my friend. Leave him alone, you silly boys!'

Daniel had been quite a clingy baby but when it was time to start playgroup he went off happily. However, within a few days the play leaders started greeting me each lunchtime with the latest tale of what he'd been up to – snatching toys off other children, unable to wait his turn at juice time and kicking out at staff when they tried to get involved.

I thought a lot of his anger and frustration might be because he was constantly tired. He tended to go to sleep very late and wake early. He was a fitful sleeper, often waking several times a night, and he started sleepwalking too – it wasn't unusual to find him sitting on the floor in front of the blank TV screen in the middle of the night. However, as he got used to the routine of playgroup he seemed to settle down, and as he approached his fourth birthday he seemed more than ready for nursery school.

With nursery came a whole new set of experiences for Daniel to get used to and he just didn't seem able to cope. The nursery was at the same school his sister, Katie, went to, so he was used to going there every day, but on the first day he seemed scared about the idea of going into the classroom and he ran away. It took several minutes to persuade him to try it out but once he was inside and saw all the toys and activities he became very excited, so I didn't worry too much about his initial reluctance.

For a few months everything went well at nursery – indeed, Daniel appeared to be something of a leader, and wherever he went, a small band of children followed. However, the tantrums and aggression soon reappeared, and if Daniel became fed up with one of his loyal fans, he would go on the attack. One day I arrived at nursery to be told he had slapped another child, apparently in frustration at not getting his own way. The staff had dealt with it firmly but I was mortified by his behaviour.

Part of the problem was that Daniel was such a headstrong character that it was very easy for him to dominate weaker children – not in a bullying way, but just because he was such a strong presence. It was decided to move him from the morning sessions to the afternoon group, where there were several other strong characters, and that seemed to make a difference, as he didn't get his way so easily with the other children after that.

His nursery teacher was fabulous and managed to keep him in check most of the time, but she did speak to me and suggest that it might be worth talking to my GP about his behaviour. That was the first time anyone had suggested that this might be something more than the average toddler tantrum phase, and that worried me.

What concerned me more were the strange obsessions Daniel was developing. We quite often went to car boot sales at the weekend. At the time he loved the TV programme *Jellikins* and one day he bought a cuddly Strum, the purple bear from the show. It didn't take long before Strum was going everywhere with us. I know kids get attached to their toys, but Daniel seemed to be almost dependent on this bear, sniffing him for comfort when he was tired or frustrated or in a new situation. Daniel's dad had given him an old PlayStation and he would have spent hours playing Medievil and Crash Bandicoot, given the chance. He also had a brief but entertaining obsession with the TV show *Only Fools and Horses*. Everyone became known as 'Rodney, you plonker' or a 'dipstick' (or 'dickstick', as three-year-old

Daniel actually said!) and I can remember him sitting back at the breakfast table one day, a big smile on his face as he uttered the classic Del Boy phrase: 'Mont Blanc!' Slightly more embarrassing was the time he told a friend of mine to 'Shut up, you tart!'

More worryingly, he became obsessed with bottoms and willies – his own and other people's. At first I thought this too was just a phase, but as time went on the nursery staff became quite concerned about this latest obsession, which they classed as 'highly sexualised behaviour'. In my eyes, it started when they looked at a book about the body in class; to the school, there had to be something deeper at its roots. To my horror, Social Services were informed and a social worker came round to our home to check that everything was OK. Happy that there were no signs of abuse or mistreatment, they retreated and the matter passed over, but it was a very distressing time for us all.

Food was another problem area. Daniel had a very limited diet and at one stage he went for a fortnight eating nothing but jam sandwiches and hot chocolate! In the greater scheme of things this wasn't a big issue – I quickly learned to pick my battles carefully – and soon enough he returned to a more normal eating pattern, but it was something else that set the alarm bells ringing.

And throughout all this the tantrums continued, bringing with them an increasing amount of violence. Daniel seemed to get angry so easily, about everything and nothing, and hit, kicked and punched anyone who got in his way – normally his sister and me, but teaching staff and other children were sometimes hurt too. I started withdrawing toys or sending him to his room as a punishment, but he just said he didn't care and proceeded to wreck his bedroom, throwing toys and clothes around and thumping the walls over and over with his tiny fists. There didn't seem to be any pattern to his mood swings either. Something that wound him up one day would seem perfectly acceptable the next.

At times I really didn't know what to do – none of the techniques that had worked with his sister, such as reward charts, Time Out and consequences, made a difference, and I was left frustrated, confused and upset, and feeling like a failure. I was also starting to get the impression that the school thought I was just a 'bad parent' – even though they knew Daniel's sister and could see she was a completely different, well-behaved child.

Eventually, I took Daniel to see our GP, who referred him to a paediatrician. If we could find a clinical reason for his behaviour, I reasoned, the nursery might be able to help him – he'd be moving into reception class soon and I didn't know how he would cope. After a brief assessment the paediatrician said yes, there were some signs that his behaviour was unusual but there was nothing concrete to suggest he had a specific problem. We came away with a vague understanding that Daniel was 'borderline ADHD' – which meant nothing really.

Infant School

Tuesday 16th March 2004: Daniel's been sent home from school. Again. This is the fourth time since last Monday.

So with this vague diagnosis of 'borderline ADHD' hanging over his head, Daniel started at the infant school on the same site as his nursery. And for a while everything was OK. His class teacher had come up with him from nursery and she already had a pretty good idea of his abilities and issues. He proved himself to be a bright and intelligent boy, popular with the other children, and when he let himself take part in lessons, he made useful contributions and was a valued member of the class.

However, it really was a case of when he let himself take part – basically, if Daniel decided he didn't want to join in, he wouldn't. And so started a pattern that was to last for many years. Daniel has always had very strong views about what he thinks is a good use of his time or something he will enjoy, and what is, in his eyes, stupid or rubbish or boring, and therefore not worth doing. For example, he has never seen the point of art. It's not something he enjoys, it's not something he is any good at – so why should he have to do it? And in a completely logical way I agree with him, but, of course, within the structure of education that argument doesn't work. He's also always had a lack of self-confidence and a real fear of failure – so choosing not to do something in the first place was a good way of avoiding the risk of failing to do it well. So school was always going to be a struggle for Daniel, even with a teacher who understood and could manage his temper, because he very much set his own agenda and seemingly chose when he would participate.

Because of the problems he'd had in nursery, Daniel started reception class on the Special Needs register at School Action level. This meant that the school was aware he was not making the expected progress and might need additional help within school, such as extra support or different teaching techniques. Coincidentally, he was also on the Able Child Register as the school recognised than in some areas, especially maths and science, he was highly intelligent!

(The Special Educational Needs process in the UK changed in 2014. I'll explain more about the new system in a later chapter, Support for Your Child in School, but School Action and School Action Plus has been replaced with SEN Support.)

Every term I attended a meeting with Daniel's class teacher and the school SENCO (Special Educational Needs Co-ordinator) to discuss his behaviour and progress and write an IEP – Individual Education Plan – which listed his targets for the coming weeks.

The school was concerned about Daniel's lack of concentration, general disobedience and increasing aggression, so partway through the year he was moved to the next level – School Action Plus – which allowed for external intervention, and he started to receive some one-to-one support in class and regular anger management sessions from the local Behaviour Support team. This seemed to be really beneficial to Daniel and he appeared much calmer generally and started to thrive in school too.

Somehow he made it to the end of reception year and I was really starting to think everything was looking up – until I discovered who his teacher would be for Year 1. She was newly qualified – not in itself a problem – but I knew her out of the school setting and knew that she had some quite difficult children herself who she seemed to struggle with almost as much as I struggled with Daniel. It was obvious that he needed someone strong and firm to manage his behaviour and this new teacher just didn't seem to be the right person for the job.

I was seriously worried that everything was going to come crashing down around us and I even spoke to the head teacher to express my concerns, but she assured me that this teacher would cope just fine. Furthermore, the school also felt that the anger management had been so successful that Daniel no longer needed it, and they withdrew the extra help he had been getting from Behaviour Support.

So Year 1 started. New teacher, new classroom, new routines. And while most children thrived in that environment, Daniel struggled to cope with all the changes and the new structure of his day. Without a teacher able to manage his behaviour, or the additional support he'd been receiving, he went completely out of control. Every day, it seemed, he was getting into trouble – attacking the other children, refusing to work, shouting at staff. His teacher kept a daily record of his behaviour and a fairly typical day was:

> Good start to the day till about 10am, which Daniel was awarded a sticker for. Playtime he became rough and banged a Year 2's head against the wall. He was dealt with appropriately by support staff. After school club: very aggressive, punched other children, punched Katie and made her nose bleed. Has hit playleader several times. Ask him to do anything and he calls people names and says, 'I'm going to kill you,' 'You're dead meat,' or 'I don't care' after everything we ask him.

At this stage, remember, Daniel didn't have a firm medical diagnosis, just a vague 'borderline ADHD' on his records, so I suppose with hindsight I can understand why, when his behaviour suddenly deteriorated, the school pointed the finger at me as the cause of the issues. My relationship with Daniel and Katie's father had broken down and we had moved out, but I was adamant that I was doing the very best I could and that Daniel's behaviour was despite my efforts, not because of them – but the school wouldn't see it that way. I had a friend whose son had ADHD and Asperger's and I could see similarities between him and Daniel, but because we'd been given no official diagnosis, the school was unwilling to consider that there could be a medical reason for his behaviour.

It became very clear, during numerous meetings, that they thought I was struggling to discipline Daniel, that his home life was chaotic and that his behaviour was due in part to my poor parenting skills. All this despite his sister, who obviously had the same home life, background and parenting, continuing to do well; in fact, she was a star pupil, both academically and behaviourally. With hindsight, I know now that all the behaviours Daniel was demonstrating were directly linked to his condition. At the time, though, it was devastating – not least because I was struggling to cope with his behaviour myself. No parent wants to believe they are failing their child, but when every day is a challenge and you have no support from the school either, it's easy to do.

So just what were the behaviour issues that were causing so much concern? We'll take a look at them in the next chapter.

ADHD Behaviours

Tuesday 6th March 2001: I'm sure Daniel's sole purpose in life is to wind me up!

You'll find information about the diagnostic criteria for ADHD in Appendix 1 at the end of the book. However, I wanted to include some practical, real-life examples of behaviours that my own ADHD child displayed, because if you're at all worried about someone you know having the condition, you might be able to relate to them.

The following are the main behaviours that were causing concern to the teachers at Daniel's infant school and me – and many of them continued to affect Daniel for many years. He's 18 now and fortunately he has found ways to manage his behaviour most of the time – although he still has challenges.

Obviously, this list is unique to my son and every child is different, but if you have any experience of dealing with ADHD, I'm sure you'll find many familiar behaviours here. Although most children show some of these symptoms from time to time, a child with ADHD is likely to behave in these ways regularly, and to a greater extent than other children.

If you are worried about your own child and recognise a handful of these behaviour patterns occurring on a regular basis, it would be well worth seeking medical advice, either for your own peace of mind or to find out if there is a problem that needs support.

Mood swings

I've often commented to people that Daniel is like Jekyll and Hyde. On a good day he is charming, funny and a pleasure to be with; but when the anger takes over, he can be a complete monster. His behaviour can be totally unpredictable and although we have learned the signs that he's close to meltdown, the trigger is not always apparent.

Temper tantrums

As Daniel got older, his toddler tantrums continued, ranging in intensity from verbal abuse and aggression to violent meltdowns. It's as if something else takes over and he has no control of it. When he's in the throes of a meltdown, he shakes with rage and even his facial expression changes. Have you ever seen one of the *Incredible Hulk* cartoons or films? That moment when Dr Bruce Banner transforms into the big green monster? That's what Daniel is like when a meltdown takes hold. It's a scary time and it's often difficult to know what to do for the best. There were times when Daniel had several meltdowns a day, several days in a row, for no discernible reason, and those days were very difficult to cope with.

Verbal abuse, name calling and backchat

Since he was quite small, Daniel has had a tendency to become quite verbally abusive, especially to adults. In some ways it's acted as a kind of pressure valve – if he's getting frustrated, it's better for him to get that anger out verbally than to become physically violent. I know that's no excuse, and Daniel has always been punished in some way for verbal abuse, but it's a case of learning to pick your battles. Over time Daniel has learned that although we don't like bad language, if it helps him relieve his anger at home, then we'd prefer that to physical aggression. However, he has also learned to control his temper more in public.

Aggression and violence

Some people think that the ADHD child works on the principle of 'Punch first, ask questions later', and although it can seem that way, I don't think that's actually what's going on. I bet we've all been in a situation where we wanted to thump someone for annoying us, but we have the built-in control not to follow through with those actions, so it appears only as a fleeting thought. In a child with ADHD, the part of the brain that controls that impulsiveness is under-stimulated, so when they feel angry enough to hit someone, there's nothing to stop that thought becoming an action. The action is often followed with remorse, either straight away, or as soon as they've calmed down, because they realise that their action was wrong – but by then it's too late. There have been many occasions where Daniel has hit or kicked someone in anger – and immediately realised what he's done and been filled with remorse.

Fearlessness

Many children with ADHD show a lack of fear, which can have serious consequences if not handled properly. Luckily, Daniel has always had a good sense of road safety, but when he was younger, he regularly wandered off, especially when we were out shopping – something would catch his eye while my back was turned and he'd disappear. I used toddler reins when he was very small, and held his hand until an unfeasibly old age, at which point it became embarrassing for both of us, and luckily he hasn't had any serious scrapes because of his desire to wander. The nearest he came to harm was when we were walking along a brook one day. I was childminding at the time and pushing a double buggy, and Daniel was walking just behind me. I turned round and he'd disappeared. After some frantic shouting I found him halfway down the bank of the stream, sitting in a clump of stinging nettles! Fortunately, no harm was done but it was a big shock, especially when I realised just how serious it could have been.

Impulsiveness

Daniel's impulsive streak showed up through wandering off or aggression and verbal abuse, and it's a common trait of ADHD. Many children and adults with ADHD act without thinking about the consequences, and depending on the situation that can have serious results – incidents of crime and car accidents are higher amongst young people with ADHD than the norm because of their impulsive nature. As a young adult, Daniel's impulsiveness means he will dive into a new situation, project or trip without thinking through the potential obstacles or outcomes, which in many ways is a really refreshing way of thinking – but, of course, it doesn't always have a happy ending! He's also very impulsive with money – if he sees something he wants and he has the money for it, he'll buy it without a second thought. For example, a while ago he decided he wanted to learn the guitar. He rushed out and spent £200 on one, even though I had an old guitar he could have used. Eighteen months later, he hasn't learned a single chord!

Inflexibility and a need for routine

One of the biggest issues we had to deal with when Daniel was younger was his need for structure and routine and his inflexibility to changing situations. For example, whereas most children would love an impromptu visit to the park, Daniel would steadfastly refuse to leave the house. The way I see it, his brain would be in one mode and he just found it very difficult to change his thinking from 'We're doing this' to 'Now we're doing that.' Although we found ways to deal with this at home (see chapter on Tips and Techniques for Dealing with ADHD), it was more problematic at school, where even the smallest change to his routine could upset him. I remember one Thursday the school phoned and asked me to collect Daniel because he had become very aggressive in class. It turned out that they usually had a maths test on Thursdays but this week it had been postponed for some reason – and that was enough to upset his equilibrium, resulting in a meltdown. Even now he struggles with change at times. In his last year at senior school, a rearrangement of the classroom furniture caused a mood change and some aggressive, defiant behaviour, which even Daniel later acknowledged was a stupid reaction.

Being easily distracted, lack of concentration and forgetfulness

These are some of the most common ADHD behaviour traits. Daniel always found it difficult to concentrate on school work for any period of time, and in a class of 30 children there were just too many distractions. Daniel was easily distracted at home too – in the mornings I'd lay out his clothes and come back later to find him standing there with one leg in and one leg out of his trousers because something more interesting had caught his attention, and at dinner time he'd often stop with the fork halfway between the plate and his mouth because he'd forgotten what he was doing! Interestingly, he can concentrate on a computer game, often for hours – the thinking is that the rapidly changing environment of a game matches the rapid movement of the brain of children with ADHD – this is why they can concentrate on a game rather than a book, which is obviously slower to change. Daniel also finds it difficult to remember more than a couple of things at a time without prompting. For instance, we recently opened a bank account for him and he walked to the bank on his own one day to pay a cheque in and ask for a balance. Well, he remembered to pay the cheque in!

Low self-esteem and self-confidence

Daniel has always suffered from low self-esteem and self-confidence, and it's something of a self-perpetuating, masochistic prophecy, I fear. When children are constantly being told off, it's easy for them to feel bad about themselves and often their way of dealing with that is to behave even more badly to get some attention – which, of course, backfires because they're told off for it, and so it continues.

Fidgeting and verbal outbursts

Another classic sign of ADHD is constant fidgeting, movement or verbal outbursts. When he was younger, Daniel found it very difficult to sit still and he tended to shout out the answers in class rather than putting his hand up and waiting. In class he would jump up and down from his seat or run around the classroom, almost like someone else was holding his remote control, and at home, even when he was absorbed in a TV programme, he would be swinging his leg or tapping his fingers. He has calmed down a lot as he's matured, but even now he constantly taps his fingers when he's bored, concentrating or distracted.

Unable to take turns

In a similar vein to the lack of control leading to fidgeting and verbal outbursts, many children with ADHD find it very difficult to take turns. We played a lot of board games when Daniel was small, and although it often led to tantrums and tears, I think it helped him learn how to be patient and wait for other people.

Fear of the unknown

As well as being unable to cope with sudden changes, Daniel has always suffered from fear of the unknown – in other words, he would rather stick with the familiar than try something new. He often covers this up by saying that the new thing will be boring and he doesn't want to do it anyway. As an example, his class was once going on a trip to a farm. He had a paediatrician appointment on the same day but I managed to rearrange it so he could go on the trip. However, Daniel was adamant that he didn't want to go, to the extent that he said he'd rather go to the clinic than the farm! Of course, he went on the trip and had a great time, as I knew he would, but the very next time a trip was offered he reverted to the 'It's boring, I don't want to go' routine. As he's got older, Daniel has learned that new experiences are normally fun, and although he often feels anxious, he's much more open to trying new things.

Defiance

Although defiance is not a symptom of ADHD, it is the major feature of ODD – Oppositional Defiant Disorder – which is one of the co-morbidities that can accompany ADHD. Since he was young, Daniel has had a tendency to only want to do the things that he wants to do, which sometimes results in outright defiance. It's especially difficult to deal with when there's the threat of a consequence or the promise of a reward for the right behaviour which is met with a firm 'I don't care' – where do you go from there?! In our case it was to tell him, 'Well, *I* care' – which quite often made him stop and think.

School phobia

The more problems Daniel had in school, the less he wanted to be there until eventually he developed some sort of school phobia. Quite literally, I would deliver him to his classroom door and he would walk through the classroom, into the corridor and out of another door into the playground before anyone noticed. As his behaviour got worse, the school responded by calling me to take him home, and he learned that if he didn't want to be at school, all he had to do was misbehave and he'd be sent home!

Lack of respect for authority

Since he was very small, Daniel hasn't seen any difference between his peer group, his family and people in positions of authority. This has caused all manner of problems, because he treats everyone the same way. He's always talked in a very grown-up way, which doesn't always go down well with adults, especially 'authority figures', because he will often question their actions and this can be seen as a lack of respect rather than a child talking to an adult on their terms. In fact, Daniel has huge respect for those people who he feels deserve it, or who show him respect in return.

Need for control

Because Daniel's behaviour so often made him feel completely out of control, he craved having control of situations because it made him feel safe. Combined with his perceived lack of respect for teachers, this meant he often tried to take control of a situation when it wasn't his place to do so. In fact, this still happens now, as he has a tendency to try to pick up on other people's poor behaviour if it is bothering him, rather than leaving it for the person in charge to deal with.

Literal understanding

Many children with ADHD also have elements of autism and Daniel is no exception. One of the ways this shows itself is through a very literal understanding of language. If I told Daniel we'd do something in two minutes, he would watch the clock and then come to me exactly two minutes later demanding my attention. He also struggled to understand phrases and idioms – for example, he'd want to know what cat and why it was in the bag anyway! This has affected life in some amusing ways. One day we were rushing to get ready for school and I asked Daniel to get his PE bag. Now, most children would automatically know I meant the bag with PE kit in it, but Daniel appeared a few minutes later, empty bag in hand, and didn't understand my frustration – after all, he'd got the PE bag, hadn't he? Another time he had homework to do and I asked him to fill in one side of the page – he came back with one sentence in very large letters, filling the entire side of paper. Well, he'd done what I asked, I guess…

Mess for the sake of it

OK, lots of children are messy – I know I was – but Daniel often seemed to make a mess just for the sake of it. I'm sure in his mind he was thinking, 'Nice neat box of puzzles? That's no good, let's throw them on the floor and mix the pieces up. Basket of toys? No, they'd be better off in the tumble dryer. Crayons? Let's grind them into the carpet – that'll be funny and I bet Mum will be really proud of me for that!'

If you have a child with ADHD, I'm sure you'll recognise a lot of those behaviours. Later in the book I'll be outlining some of the tips and techniques that I have tried over the years that have made our lives a little easier.

OK, where were we? Ah, that's right. Daniel's infant school was as concerned about his behaviour as I was, but wasn't willing to look beyond my 'bad parenting' as a cause, which really hurt. I strongly believe that their view that it was all down to Daniel's home life played a big part in the support they did – or, rather, didn't – offer him, which had serious consequences both for Daniel and the school further down the line.

But back to the story. It's school Year 1 and Daniel has a teacher who I don't have much confidence in and little additional support – the one-to-one support and anger management training had been withdrawn, supposedly because he was managing so well. As Daniel's behaviour became worse and worse, I pleaded with the school to contact Behaviour Support and ask them to work with him again, but my pleas went unheard. Instead, the school's response to Daniel's increasingly aggressive behaviour was to send him home – I lost count of the number of times I had to drop everything and pick him up in the middle of the day. I've since found out that these 'informal exclusions' are actually illegal – but more on that later.

At the start of the summer term, and increasingly worried about Daniel's behaviour, I saw my GP again and asked for a referral back to the paediatrician who had given the 'borderline ADHD' diagnosis two years earlier. I also arranged a meeting with the school, who updated Daniel's Individual Education Plan and put in place a Pastoral Care Plan – a document that looks at the child's overall wellbeing rather than just academic issues. During the meeting I suggested that, given that

Daniel still seemed to be failing to achieve under School Action Plus, perhaps it would be worth applying for a statutory assessment for a Statement of Educational Needs (now known as an EHC Plan – more on that later, in the Support for Your Child in School chapter). I didn't know much about the system but had done some limited research and knew that a statutory assessment was the next stage and that, if a Statement was granted, it would result in additional funding for the school to increase the support Daniel received. However, the head teacher actually laughed at the suggestion and said there was no way he would qualify for a Statement. However, she did concede that they needed to do something, and offered to put in a new referral to Behaviour Support. Unfortunately, this referral got lost in the system and the school failed to follow it up until July – by which time it was too late.

Two weeks from the end of summer term, following a major meltdown where Daniel – aged six – lost his temper and threw a chair across the classroom, narrowly missing the teacher, the school issued a fixed-term, two-week exclusion. A meeting was arranged during the holidays to discuss his return to school but in the meeting it was agreed by the teaching staff – but not the Behavioural Support team – that the best way to get him the help he needed was to permanently exclude him. And I, knowing no different, agreed.

Exclusion Number One and the PRU

Thursday 16th September 2004: I'm too embarrassed to tell people Daniel's been excluded. That just doesn't happen to families like ours.

In my mind, exclusions weren't something that happened to nice families like ours; they were something you hear about in rough areas with 'bad' children. Yet when offered exclusion as the only chance that Daniel would receive the help he so obviously needed, I was quick to take it. What other option did I have?

As it turned out, there was a wealth of things the school could have done, but when you're thrown into a situation that you don't fully understand, you take whatever you can get. So it was arranged that Daniel would attend the local Pupil Referral Unit – which, very conveniently, was located just over the road from our home.

Better known as a PRU, these small units are designed to accept children who can't access mainstream education for a variety of reasons. Often the children are there because, like Daniel, they have severe emotional or behavioural difficulties that have led to exclusion. However, children can also be sent to a PRU because they have an unstable home life, have been out of school for a long time with illness or because they are at risk of committing crime if they remain in mainstream schools – perhaps because they are bullies. (Conversely, children have also been known to attend a PRU because they have been the victim of bullies…which doesn't seem right to me.)

Anyway, Daniel started at our local PRU on a part-time basis, at first only a couple of mornings a week but gradually building up to four days a week, morning and afternoon sessions. There were only three children in the primary unit with two teachers and a teaching assistant, and on the whole he settled in quickly and responded well to the small group setting.

Work was set in manageable chunks, and learning in that way seemed to suit Daniel. He also responded well to the PRU's reward system – children could earn a maximum of four stickers each session for everything from good academic work to doing the right thing to owning up to bad behaviour. Twenty stickers gained a chocolate bar or 50p towards a shopping voucher, with a further £2 voucher for each completed book (60 stickers).

One of the issues the staff at the PRU set out to tackle was the breaking of cycles of behaviour that Daniel had got himself into. I already mentioned that he had learned that bad behaviour often resulted in him being sent home, and he did play on that a lot at his school, so when the PRU threatened to send him home one day, I was horrified that the same cycle would begin again. Instead, they found other ways to punish him for violent behaviour, including withholding treats such as music lessons, or ignoring behaviour as far as possible until he realised that his tantrum wasn't going to achieve anything.

So the PRU seemed to be working out for Daniel, but I was still angry that it had taken a permanent exclusion to get him the help he needed, and I started digging around to see if there could have been an alternative. I'd strongly recommend that if you find yourself in a situation where your child could be heading for an exclusion, you do your research and arm yourself to the teeth with all the information you can find – because what I discovered really shocked me.

Daniel's (first) permanent exclusion took place in 2004 when the Local Education Authorities (LEAs) managed schools. Since then this has been taken over by Local Authorities (LAs), but other than the change from LEA to LA the guidance is still much the same now.

First, it turned out that all those days when Daniel had been sent home early were illegal. If a school wants to exclude a child, even for an afternoon, it has to be done properly, as a fixed-term exclusion, with details being recorded in a log and paperwork filled in, specifying the exact reasons for the exclusion. Schools can't just send children home as and when they feel like it.

Second, Daniel's exclusion probably shouldn't have happened – it's as simple as that. According to government guidelines on exclusion at the time, if a child had a Statement of Needs or was on School Action or Action Plus, 'schools should try every practicable means to maintain the pupil in school, including seeking LA and other professional advice and support...or, where appropriate, asking the LA to consider carrying out a statutory assessment.'

New guidelines came out in February 2015 but children with disabilities are still offered some protection. The guidelines now say:

> The decision to exclude a pupil must be lawful, reasonable and fair. Schools have a statutory duty not to discriminate against pupils on the basis of protected characteristics, such as disability or race. Schools should give particular consideration to the fair treatment of pupils from groups who are vulnerable to exclusion.

If the school knows your child has a diagnosis of ADHD, they must not discriminate against them because of their disability.

There are a couple of other sections in the government guidance on exclusion that might be useful to you if this is a situation your child is facing. I've included a link to the guidance in Appendix 3, but bookmark the following two paragraphs for future reference!

> Early intervention to address underlying causes of disruptive behaviour should include an assessment of whether appropriate provision is in place to support any SEN or disability that a pupil may have. Head

teachers should also consider the use of a multi-agency assessment for pupils who demonstrate persistent disruptive behaviour. Such assessments may pick up unidentified special educational needs but the scope of the assessment could go further, for example, by seeking to identify mental health or family problems.

And:

Where a school has concerns about the behaviour, or risk of exclusion, of a child with additional needs, a pupil with a statement of SEN or a looked after child it should, in partnership with others (including the local authority as necessary), consider what additional support or alternative placement may be required. This should involve assessing the suitability of provision for a pupil's SEN. Where a pupil has a statement of SEN, schools should consider requesting an early annual review or interim/emergency review.

In other words, if your child's behaviour is causing problems in school, the school must look at reviewing existing support, providing more support, applying for an assessment or looking for an alternative school before they consider exclusion.

In our case, the school had breached the guidance by rejecting my request for a statutory assessment and not considering any option other than exclusion. But what other options could there have been? Plenty, as it goes.

As an early measure, something as simple as moving a child to a different class can be a solution. In Daniel's case, I believe a lot of his problems stemmed from the inability of the Year 1 teacher to get a firm hold on his behaviour, and I'd stressed my opinion to the head teacher on many occasions, to no avail. To think that a simple change of class teacher could have made a difference really upsets me – that should have been the first thing they tried, before considering other options.

There are a host of external agencies that schools can and should involve in the care plan of a child with special needs, and there doesn't have to be a Statement of Educational Needs or an Education, Health and Care Plan in place to access this support. For example, every local authority has an educational psychologist experienced in dealing with issues including ADHD and autistic spectrum disorders, who can be called on for advice. Every county also has a Child and Adolescent Mental Health Service (CAMHS), which is equipped to provide a range of support tools including anger management and counselling, and schools can refer children to CAMHS or request that a member of the team comes into school to help with individual care plans.

Daniel's record did show that he had been 'mentioned' to the educational psychologist – but no more than that. Surely if a child is behaving badly enough to warrant exclusion, a referral to the Ed Psych service would be a priority? Not in the eyes of this school. And, of course, there's also Behaviour Support, who were involved with Daniel during reception year but withdrawn because he seemed to be improving – and then not contacted again until it was too late.

If the school really felt they couldn't continue to have Daniel attending on a regular basis, they could have contacted the PRU and arranged for him to attend the unit, either for a few sessions a week alongside school or on a full-time, temporary basis. This would have ensured that Daniel stayed in mainstream education while gaining additional support for his behaviour, and the school would have had some respite in the meantime. But that wasn't offered to us unless we accepted permanent exclusion.

Finally, schools can arrange a 'managed move' to another school, either as a preventative measure or an alternative to exclusion. Again, this would mean the school was no longer responsible for Daniel, but equally he wouldn't have the stigma of an exclusion on his record, and this could have been another option worth exploring – but it took my own research to find this option even existed. In fact, prior to his exclusion I had become so frustrated with the situation that I'd contacted all the local schools with a view to moving Daniel myself, but they all said the school he was at was the best one for children with needs such as his!

However, not content with ruining Daniel's academic progress through excluding him rather than considering other options, it became evident that the school had also failed to follow the strict procedure that surrounds exclusions. Schools are supposed to notify parents and the local authority of a permanent exclusion 'without delay', both when the exclusion is originally decided and after the governors have accepted the decision. In our case it took six weeks for us to receive a letter and the local authority's Exclusion Officer only found out because I called him! Fortunately, Daniel's place at the PRU had already been arranged so his education didn't suffer as a result, but in a different situation he could have risked being lost in the system altogether.

With research under my belt and evidence in hand that the school had let Daniel down completely, I went along to the Governors' Discipline Panel meeting, ready to do battle. This meeting has to be held before any exclusion can be signed off and it's meant to be an opportunity for parents to state the case for their child in an unbiased environment. However, in my experience (and I've been through it twice now) the governors will always come down on the side of the school, no matter what the evidence.

And so, despite me taking along a huge document outlining all the options open to the school that they'd ignored and their failure to comply with the procedure, the exclusion was upheld.

Exclusion Tribunal

I wasn't prepared to leave it at that, though. Armed with my evidence of the school's failure to consider all the options and follow procedure, I decided to appeal against the decision to exclude. I didn't want Daniel to go back to that school – too much had happened to make that feasible – but I didn't feel that he should carry the stigma of exclusion for mistakes made by the school, either.

On advice from SENDIST (Special Educational Needs and Disability Tribunal – details in Appendix 3: Resources) and with the support of the exclusions officer, I attended a tribunal hearing, which turned out to be a complete farce. I'm sure some parents must have a terrible time getting justice for their children in these circumstances, but luckily for me Daniel's ex-school let themselves down badly.

Rather than Daniel's class teacher, or the SENCO, or the head teacher appearing, the school sent along two governors – neither of whom had been at the Discipline

Panel meeting – who knew nothing of the circumstances surrounding the exclusion. And where I had a carefully prepared statement of my evidence, they had Daniel's entire school record – which included reading charts, leaflets on bullying, blank incident report forms and a loose-leaf version of the entire school prospectus! Finally, the school's spokesperson managed to find their prepared statement from among the dozens of pages of completely irrelevant information, but they were unable to answer any of the questions put to them by the tribunal judges, the exclusions officer or myself.

During the hearing it was revealed that as well as ignoring the government guidance on alternatives to exclusions, failing to follow procedure and handing out more than 20 illegal 'unofficial exclusions', the school had also failed to keep a log of incidents, as required by law. Worse still, the governors who upheld the head teacher's decision to exclude did so based not on Daniel's school record but on a brief statement written by the head teacher. In fact, they hadn't even seen his school record prior to the tribunal!

I left the tribunal feeling optimistic and sure enough, two days later I received a letter that stated:

After careful consideration of your representations and those of the school and the Exclusions Officer, and in the light of all available evidence, the Panel has decided that it is not practical to direct Daniel's reinstatement, although otherwise reinstatement would have been appropriate... Your child's record will show that the permanent exclusion was overturned on appeal.

Exclusion overturned – music to my ears.

Oh, and there was more. It turned out that had Daniel already been diagnosed with ADHD, the school could have been in breach of the Disability Discrimination Act too.

We'd won justice for Daniel…but at a price.

Diagnosis, Diet and Medication

Friday 6th May 2005: Daniel's on drugs. And I'm really pleased.

While the exclusion appeal process was rumbling on, my doctor arranged a referral for Daniel to see the paediatrician again – and this time we came away with a proper diagnosis. Referring to information supplied by the Pupil Referral Unit staff on a Connors Rating Scale – which lists certain behaviours that are seen in a variety of spectrum disorders and asks whether they are seen rarely, sometimes or often – he examined Daniel thoroughly and decided that there was indeed a medical cause for his behaviour. The diagnosis was Attention Deficit Hyperactivity Disorder with secondary Oppositional Defiant Disorder and autistic traits. So not only did Daniel have ADHD, Combined, and a common co-morbidity, ODD, he was also firmly on the autistic spectrum, mainly because of his literal understanding of language and poor social skills.

At last his condition had a label. I know a lot of parents are terrified of labelling their kids for fear of the repercussions, but this was the best possible news for me. Finally, I knew that his behaviour wasn't due to my parenting skills or our family background but because of a genuine genetic disorder! Perhaps the best thing about having a firm diagnosis is that once you know what you are dealing with, you can start to find suitable treatments.

Because Daniel was only seven, the paediatrician was reluctant to prescribe medication straight away – a decision I initially agreed with – and he also felt that because Daniel's diagnosis included autistic traits, medication such as Ritalin might not actually make a difference. Instead, we decided to take a look at Daniel's diet.

You may remember that at one stage Daniel had existed on nothing but jam sandwiches and hot chocolate. Fortunately, his tastes had widened slightly since then, but as a single parent on a limited budget I did tend to rely a little too heavily on chicken nuggets and chips. I made a concerted effort to cook more food from scratch and I also tried some exclusion diets – first wheat, then dairy. It was difficult to impose on an already angry and difficult child, and I maybe didn't give each regime long enough to work, but it was clear after a couple of months of following special diets that there was no discernible difference to his behaviour at all. The tantrums and aggression and defiance continued.

There is a theory that the symptoms of ADHD can be improved by boosting the brain with omega 3 fish oils, so for a while I tried giving Daniel supplements. He refused to take the fishy oil on a spoon, so for a few weeks I surreptitiously sneaked it into his dinners. Poor boy – I think he was very confused about why everything from spaghetti Bolognese to pancakes tasted slightly of fish! Eventually, he caught me red-handed dripping the oil on his food, so that was the end of that little wheeze. I then found a fish oil supplement in a strawberry suspension; Daniel was very fond of Nestlé's strawberry milk at the time, so I added some of the supplement to that, but again he caught me one day and refused to drink it ever again! Perhaps if I'd been able to spoon-feed him a couple of teaspoons a day, the omega 3 might have had a positive effect on his behaviour, but as it was I didn't notice any direct benefit. That's not to say it isn't worth trying, though – in fact, if you are concerned about your child's behaviour but don't have a diagnosis, anything is worth a go.

I'd started noticing a link between the sweets and drinks that Daniel consumed and his behaviour, so food colourings were the next thing I looked at. The paediatrician agreed that artificial colourings had been linked to hyperactivity, aggression and poor concentration, and he gave me a list of specific E-numbers to avoid. Although I thought I'd been careful to buy brands free from artificial additives, it turned out that the squash Daniel usually drank had one of these colourings in it – Sunset Yellow – and I couldn't be sure about drinks he had while out and about. For example, his sister went to a dance class once a week and I helped at the tuck shop, which sold those Panda 'cup' drinks that came in lurid colours and, on checking, were full of E numbers. Sometimes Daniel would have one of these drinks and although his behaviour was pretty dreadful anyway, we'd suddenly see a huge explosion of aggression or a meltdown of enormous proportions. Could there be a link?

For weeks I checked every label, every packet, and I made sure that not a single E number passed Daniel's lips. And while the general bad behaviour continued unabated, I did notice that the frequency and severity of the most violent outbursts did recede somewhat. Since then we have tried very hard to exclude colourings, and although it wasn't a solution in itself, I'm sure it has made a difference.

Proof of my theory about artificial colours came one summer when Daniel sneaked a bottle of his favourite Fanta Fruit Twist drink, which he knew he wasn't allowed because it contained E102. Within minutes of finishing the drink he had a Hulk-like explosion of rage totally out of proportion to the event that triggered it, and in stark contrast to the unusually angelic behaviour that had preceded it! Fortunately, Fanta changed the recipe of Fruit Twist a few years later so Daniel can now drink it without it having any ill effects on his behaviour.

Medication

Four months into Daniel's time at the Pupil Referral Unit the novelty was starting to wear off and his behaviour again began to deteriorate. He frequently refused to go into the unit, or would leave partway through the morning – it being directly opposite our house was handy in some ways, but it also meant Daniel felt he could come home whenever he felt like it. When he was in class, he was aggressive, rude and violent – the meltdowns came frequently and he would often kick out or throw objects at his teachers. They all agreed that he was a bright boy but he seemed unwilling to want to learn, even with the more manageable lesson structure and the reward system. And he thought the other children were 'stupid'.

Considering this was meant to be the best placement for him, I was beginning to despair. We had a structured life at home with rules and boundaries and rewards and punishments, none of which seemed to make a difference. And I'd tried all the exclusion diets and supplements I could cope with. I was ready for something else – medication.

Now, I know the idea of medicating kids with ADHD tends to polarise folk. Many people feel that drugs such as Ritalin simply zombify our over-energetic youngsters; others believe parents go to the doctor for Ritalin because they can't be bothered with proper parenting. Medication is not for everyone, and it doesn't work for everyone. And at first I was very reluctant to try medication for Daniel because, after all, what parent does want their child to be taking strong mind-altering drugs?

However, I started thinking about it rationally. If my son had epilepsy or asthma, I wouldn't think twice about giving him the medication he needed to control the condition. Why was ADHD any different? After all, it is a genuine medical condition, with biological roots – and if medication could help him have the control to manage his behaviour, then I'd be denying him the chance of a more normal life if I didn't let him try it.

I did plenty of research into the pros and cons and decided to talk to Daniel's paediatrician about it at our next appointment. Unfortunately, he'd been called away on an emergency and a locum was taking his clinic. I told the locum all about the exclusion and the unit and how worried I was about Daniel's behaviour, and he made lots of notes and said yes, medication did look like the right option but he wasn't willing to prescribe drugs to another doctor's patient. We had to make another appointment to see the paediatrician – but the next one wasn't for two months. This time our paediatrician was ill, so again we saw a locum who recommended we just continue with the additive-free diet. I felt despondent because although I could see a difference in Daniel's behaviour, it was still affecting both school and home life; he still had meltdowns, he was still defiant, and life was still very difficult for us all. Eventually, eight months after our first appointment we managed to see our paediatrician and he agreed to prescribe a low dosage of ADHD medication, to see how it went.

The first drug Daniel tried was Concerta. This is a slow-release, long-acting version of the drug methylphenidate, and the hope was that one low-dosage tablet would last all day, helping Daniel both at school and at home in the evening. Unfortunately, the tablets were huge and he found it impossible to swallow them, so I called the clinic who arranged for us to pick up some

Ritalin tablets – Ritalin is the more commonly known brand name for methylphenidate but it is shorter-acting, in and out of the bloodstream in a few hours. The tablets were much smaller, and although Daniel still couldn't manage to swallow them, I was given permission to crush them and give him them on a spoonful of yoghurt, and he was able to take it this way.

Daniel was only given a very low dose – 10mg – but the transformation was amazing. Within about 15 minutes of taking the medication, you could physically see him relax and calm down. Mornings in our house were normally a nightmare, with Daniel bouncing off the walls while I tried to get us all organised, but suddenly he was more calm and attentive and cooperative, and that seemed to last for a few hours – until the medication wore off. Evenings were still a nightmare, but as long as he could make it through the school day, I was happy.

Indeed, he was doing much better at school as a result of taking the Ritalin. In my diary I wrote:

> We have seen an effect – a really positive one. Daniel has had the most fantastic week at school; he's had maximum effort stickers every day; he's been described as cooperative and considerate and thoughtful; he's done handwriting and comprehension and other tasks he normally refuses point blank to try, and he has been a much more happy boy overall – and he says that himself. It's early days and this could be just a coincidence or some sort of placebo effect we're seeing – but whatever it is, we have a new improved Daniel and I think this could be the making of him.

In fact, the medication had such a positive effect on Daniel that the Pupil Referral Unit soon decided it was time for him to be reintegrated into mainstream school. We were due to move house – and county – during the summer holidays, and it was important that Daniel was ready and able to start a new school once we'd moved, so the PRU arranged for him to attend a Year 2 class at a small school with an autistic unit attached, one morning a week. He loved it and seemed to settle in really well, so gradually the mornings were increased until by the end of the summer term he had completed two weeks of full-time, mainstream school. Finally, things were looking up.

Medication has had its downsides. Ritalin is a known appetite suppressant and Daniel's appetite was not good when he was taking the tablets. He rarely ate lunch and by the evening, when the medication had started to wear off, he was often starving, regularly having a large bowl of cereal before bed despite eating a big dinner. His height and weight, as well as his blood pressure, were monitored every six months at our regular CAMHS appointments, and he's always been underweight, but not enough to worry hugely about. There's also a risk that Ritalin can suppress growth, but as Daniel is now six feet tall that's not affected him! However, it also acts as a depressant to an extent, and I have heard some dreadful stories of children becoming depressed and threatening suicide. Fortunately, Daniel wasn't affected that badly, but he does feel the medication dampened his mood, although he also knows the benefits outweighed the side-effects.

I'm going to jump ahead a bit in the story now. As Daniel grew, the Ritalin, which only stays active for five or six hours, started to wear off more quickly, so a small lunchtime dose was added, which really helped keep him focused during the afternoons. The dosage increased gradually over the years as Daniel grew bigger, and it made a huge difference to his life. However, he still struggled at times and we have had some major issues which seemed to coincide with the times when his medication was altered – which you'll read about in the next chapter.

Junior School

Monday 13th February 2006: Daniel seems to have become a role model for some of the less well-behaved boys at his school. Amazing! So long as he has his medication he is a lovely, sweet, kind boy. Hurray!

In 2005 we moved house and county and Daniel started afresh at a new school. Because of all the upheaval he'd had since his exclusion, I spent a lot of time looking at the available schools to try to find the one that would work best for him.

We were moving to a small village and I first looked at the school there. It was quite a large one, which in itself wasn't a problem, but I was concerned by the head teacher's attitude. I told her all about Daniel and his history and she didn't seem overly interested in his case – until I mentioned he was on medication. She made a big deal of it and said I would have to go into school every day to give him his tablet because her staff couldn't. I explained several times that at that time he only had it in the mornings, but she didn't seem to listen, and I decided this wasn't going to be the right environment for him.

It's well worth being aware of the law in this area. Medication is always the responsibility of the parent, and schools have no legal duty to take over; they cannot be directed to give medication. They can – and usually do – give prescribed medication voluntarily, as long as staff members (usually the school nurse) have appropriate training, medication is stored securely, written instructions are provided by the parent and the medication is supplied in the original packaging. However, schools cannot discriminate against a child because of their disability, so if a school refuses them a place because they need to take medication at lunchtime and a parent isn't available to come in every day to give them it, there may be a case under the Disability Discrimination Act.

If you encounter issues with schools not wanting to give ADHD medication, ask initially to see their Medication Policy. I doubt there's a school in the country that doesn't have students who need to use their asthma inhaler regularly, or take medication for epilepsy or another condition. A quick read of the policy will help you decide whether or not they have a case to refuse to give your child their meds – and if they don't have a policy, they should.

I visited a few other schools and eventually settled on one about 15 minutes' drive away. It was a small primary school with about 90 children across six mixed-ability classes; the head teacher spoke very positively about their special needs support and it felt right.

Daniel settled into Year 3 quickly and for almost the whole of the first year he did very well. The teaching staff were aware of his diagnosis and placed him on the School Action level of needs so he could get extra support within school. We had meetings every six weeks to discuss his progress and set his Individual Education Plan (IEP) targets for the next half term.

Because Daniel had spent most of Year 2 at the Pupil Referral Unit, he hadn't done his KS2 SATS so the school ran some assessments to see where he was academically and the outcome was good, although there were some concerns about his writing and spelling. The school arranged a dyslexia assessment, which came back negative, so they started him on an accelerated learning programme to help him with phonics. Given our experience of mainstream school to date, I was really impressed with the support he was getting here, and he also seemed to be responding well.

Daniel made a few friends in school and he also joined the football team in our village and seemed to be getting on well with some of the boys there. Finally, we seemed to be experiencing some sort of normal life.

By Easter, though, the old behaviours started creeping back – but only in the afternoons. Daniel's teacher noticed his behaviour was worse after lunch and he was struggling at the after-school club he attended too. Because we'd moved counties, we had a new paediatrician, who was very supportive, and she recommended adding a lunchtime dose of Ritalin to help him get through the day.

It did help – but only after we'd been through two weeks of tantrums, aggression and disobedience the likes of which I hadn't seen for several months. I'm sure it wasn't just a coincidence – I think the extra medication actually unbalanced Daniel's system and affected his behaviour quite severely. Eventually, however, he seemed to adjust to the new drug regime, his behaviour stabilised throughout the day and he had a good summer term.

Year 4 started promisingly, but within a couple of weeks we had yet more problems. The after-school club Daniel attended started finding his behaviour more and more difficult to cope with. Although the additional medication he took at lunchtime helped him get through the school day, it was wearing off by the time he arrived at the club, and he was becoming increasingly aggressive towards the other children. He was given a final warning: one more incident of violent behaviour and he would be out.

I could completely understand where they were coming from, but it threw me into a state of panic too. At the time I was working in a well-paid full-time job, but without the after-school childcare I really didn't know whether I'd be able to carry on working, so I started researching the options. Family and friends offered to help out in the short term, if need be, but I needed a more permanent solution.

I contacted a few childminders, but as soon as I mentioned that Daniel had ADHD I could hear the shutters coming down – understandably. Most childminders just aren't equipped to deal with special needs and they were unwilling to take a chance on caring for my boy, even for a couple of hours a day.

There was another school locally that had its own after-school club, so I thought about moving Daniel there – but I was reluctant to cause him yet more upheaval, especially as he was so settled in school, and what were the chances that he'd actually manage to behave at this new club anyway? I considered giving up work completely and looking for something else, either part-time or freelance, that would fit into the school day, but there wasn't much around at the time.

Eventually, I spoke to my boss about the chance of changing my shifts, should the inevitable happen, and she seemed fairly receptive to the idea. Good job really, because that very day I picked Daniel up from the after-school club to be told he'd got into a fight with another child over a football, pulled their hair and wouldn't be welcome there again. After a panicky phone call with my boss, I was able to rearrange my working week to fit around school hours – a combination of shorter days, evening shifts and one long day when a friend picked Daniel up from school. It took a while to get used to and it affected my relationship with work colleagues, who felt I was getting special treatment. I guess I learned that you must always keep your options open because the unpredictable nature of ADHD means you can never be sure what's on the horizon.

Fortunately, despite the trouble at the after-school club, Daniel was having a good term at school. He went on a trip to a farm and despite his expectations that it was going to be 'boring' (a self-preservation technique, as explained in the ADHD Behaviours chapter) he had a great time. He was on the school football team and starting to make friends in class. He even had a few friends round for his ninth birthday party, which was a rare occurrence as throughout infant school parents had been wary about letting their children come round to play.

Of course, good times never seem to last for Daniel, and shortly before the end of the year he had a major meltdown and ended up getting into a fight, destroying someone's water bottle and threatening to strangle a girl – all over an argument in the playground. The head teacher – also Daniel's class teacher – called me into school and said that she was getting close to the point of having to exclude him because she couldn't risk the safety of the other children – but she could also see that Daniel had potential, because when he was calm, he was sensible, intelligent, hard-working and caring. Always the Jekyll and Hyde!

After everything we'd been through up to now, this was a major blow. I finally thought we'd found somewhere that could cope with Daniel and where he felt comfortable and could settle down – and it looked like it was all going to fall apart again. And this time Daniel knew there was a problem too. 'I just keep flipping, I don't know why. I'm going to end up with no friends,' he told me.

We arranged an emergency trip to the paediatrician, who agreed to increase the Ritalin dose – at the time, Daniel was on half the 'normal' dose for someone of his age and size. The school also decided to move him from School Action to School Action Plus so they could call on external support if need be. Panic over – for now, at least.

And for the next six or so months it did seem that things were improving. Almost overnight, Daniel the boy who hated school became Daniel the boy who couldn't get enough of it! One February morning we had heavy snowfall and I was concerned about the drive to school, which was down a narrow country lane. When I suggested we might not go, Daniel said, 'Oh no! If school's open, I've got to go – I want to learn extra maths and it's Thursday, ICT day!' This from the boy who'd done anything to get out of school not so long ago!

With the increased medication, Daniel's behaviour stabilised, and as well as performing well academically he was able to join in lots of activities at school. One day they had a jazz musician in for a music workshop and as usual, because it was something new and unknown, Daniel decided it was going to be boring – but he had a wonderful day, and when the school held a concert to demonstrate their singing skills, his voice could be heard clearly above everyone else's!

He also went on his first residential trip: three days and two nights at an activity centre about 20 minutes' drive away. The school had – understandably – been concerned about taking Daniel on this trip, but his improved behaviour convinced them to take a risk and he had a wonderful time; he even sent a letter home to tell me how much fun he was having!

Daniel seemed to be maturing and getting a grip on his behaviour; he was learning techniques to help him deal with his temper and academically he was coming along in leaps and bounds. His behaviour at home was better too and life was finally starting to be enjoyable. But it wasn't to last.

In July 2007 the tantrums returned, first at home, then at school too. Daniel would lose his temper over something and nothing and rage for hours, shaking from head to foot with anger. He started lashing out at anyone who strayed across his path, and we all started treading on eggshells around him. One day he threatened to stab me with a pair of scissors and then told me he didn't want to live with us any more – he said he was 'done' with people and wanted to go into care for a week. He seemed to think that he could pick and choose where he lived, and that if he went into the care system, he could come home whenever he wanted. At one stage in the argument I even picked up the phone and called Social Services – knowing full well it was the evening and they'd be closed – and let him hear the answerphone message. The following morning, calm again, he apologised and said of course he didn't want to leave home, but it was incredibly hurtful at the time. At school, his teacher said he'd started getting annoyed about things he'd coped fine with a few months earlier, and she felt perhaps his medication was no longer working so effectively. We organised another emergency appointment at the CAMHS (Child and Adolescent Mental Health Services) clinic and his medication dosage was increased again – with disastrous consequences.

It turned out that for some reason Daniel had been spitting out his medication for the last few weeks – which explained the change in his behaviour. The day the new dosage was introduced I stood over him while he took it – and the effect of going from no medication to a larger dose was dramatic. At lunchtime I was called in to collect him from school as Daniel had had a major meltdown and wrecked a classroom. The teacher had managed to get all the children out because there was a real fear for their safety as he was throwing equipment and furniture round the room. When I arrived, he threw a chair at me, then ran out of the school and up the road into the village. He refused to get into the car to come home with me, and after two hours of cajoling, talking and crying, the school called the police, and two officers arrived to talk to Daniel. Eventually, they managed to talk him down and he came home, calm, apologetic and remorseful.

The outcome was that Daniel was given a ten-day fixed-term exclusion – which effectively meant he wouldn't be back in school until the new school year. I was devastated, especially given that it seemed very reminiscent of his last exclusion, when a fixed-term exclusion had become permanent over the holidays. However, the head teacher promised that Daniel would be welcomed back in September, that they would put extra support in place (including additional special needs training for his teachers) and our paediatrician also offered some one-to-one support. Daniel was allowed to go in one afternoon to apologise to his classmates and meet his new teacher, and the school supplied him with some work to do over the next ten days – but it still felt like we were back at square one.

At first Daniel responded well to being educated at home, but very quickly he became bored and frustrated and that, of course, made his already bad behaviour even worse. On one occasion he dropped some Yu Gi Oh cards in a puddle and instantly lost his temper, coming at me with the tin he kept them in and cutting my head in the process. Fortunately, the cut wasn't too bad, but his shock at seeing blood pouring down my face was palpable. It didn't stop him from raging in his bedroom for hours, though, smashing up the room while he yelled that I was pathetic to be upset about it and that he'd rather be in care than live with me. The incident was perhaps the worst we've ever had at home, and I was seriously scared of what my nine-year-old child was capable of doing. It was time to call in some help.

We went back to see the paediatrician, who made a couple of recommendations – a parenting course for me, and some anger management counselling for Daniel. I was pretty sure that I wasn't in need of help with parenting, per se, but I did feel I was starting to lose control of Daniel in his wilder moments, so I agreed to give the course a go. The problem was I knew what Daniel was capable of – in many ways I was actually scared of him, so I was starting to back off and give in to him rather than induce a meltdown. The parenting class helped to some extent, but many of the techniques they offered were not suitable for a child with special needs, so its benefits were limited.

Daniel agreed to try the anger management counselling too – but the very first session was a disaster as he refused to get into the car to go, screamed 'Let me out!' all the way there, kicked the back of my seat constantly and caused me to stop the car – at which point he got out and started walking home! Eventually, he did get back into the car, but I had to call the clinic and apologise for our absence, and that was that – over before it even started.

After a slightly stressful summer, September rolled into view and Daniel went back to school, both to his relief and mine. Daniel had never had much in the way of homework in the past, but now that he was in Year 5 and working towards SATs he started bringing some home most weeks – and it was a constant battle to get him to do it.

Worse, he was starting to refuse to do any work at school either. He was in a new classroom, with a new teacher, and that had really unsettled him. He would often come home with that day's worksheets in his bag with instructions to complete them and bring them back the next day. I had to use every tool in my armoury to persuade him to do them, but what worked best was taking away the lead for his beloved PlayStation until the sheets were complete. After an hour or more of raging and aggression he'd finally get on with the work, but it meant our house most evenings was a stressful place.

A further visit to the paediatrician resulted in a change of medication. Up until now Daniel had been having fast-acting Ritalin, but the new prescription was for Equasym XL, a slow-release tablet. The idea was that it would stay in Daniel's system for longer, meaning he'd be able to get through school and the early part of the evening too. At least, that was the hope – and for the first week or so everything seemed to be going well, but sadly the effects didn't seem to be as long-lasting as promised. Daniel started getting into fights at school – in part because some of the other children could see how easy he was to wind up and deliberately set out to upset him. Just before the school broke up for the Christmas holidays, the head teacher called me in to warn me that they were coming very close to having to exclude him.

The new term didn't start well, as we received news that a boy at the school, who Daniel got on well with, had died in a tragic accident over the holidays. Everyone was upset and unsettled, and I think I expected Daniel to play up a bit as a result – but not as much as he did. One morning the school called to ask if he'd had his medication because he was being very disruptive and aggressive; he had, but they still asked me to bring him home for the rest of the day and he wasn't allowed back for a couple of days. In the meantime, they contacted Behaviour Support and the educational psychologist to see if there was anything else they could put in place to help Daniel in school. I was pleased they were so keen to try to help him, but I had a feeling that things were coming to a head…and I was right.

One Wednesday afternoon in January 2008 the school phoned and asked me to go in as a matter of urgency. When I arrived, I found Daniel in the head teacher's office with three members of staff. He'd had a row with some boy over a game of tag and chased him into the school, finally ending up in this office. Staff, concerned for the other boy's safety, had removed him through an adjoining door, and then stayed in the room with Daniel to try to calm him down. Instead, he had thrown everything off the desk, kicked over the chair and bin and tried to kick his way out of the door. He'd also screamed, shouted and lashed out at everyone in the room. It was rather like poking a tiger with a stick and then standing in the cage with him – you know it's only going to end in disaster.

Eventually, I persuaded the school to let me take Daniel home – even though he was still raging – and after an hour I managed to get him into the car. Once he had calmed down, we had a long chat and Daniel revealed that for the last couple of weeks he hadn't been taking his tablet; he didn't like the taste of it, he found it difficult to swallow and he'd been spitting it out in the downstairs loo when I wasn't looking. That explained why his behaviour had been so bad since the return to school – and also, in part, why this huge meltdown had occurred. That morning, suspicious that he might have been doing exactly that, I had watched him take the tablet. Having such a comparably huge dose after two weeks of nothing had thrown his system into chaos once again, resulting in some of the most violent behaviour we'd ever seen.

Later that afternoon the head teacher called to say they were excluding Daniel for four days. In my diary that night I wrote, 'Daniel keeps telling me how rubbish his life is and how useless he is. He made me cry. I've tried telling him we're all on his side and want to help him, but he has to let us.'

Exclusion Number Two, a Brush with the Law and Home Tutoring

Monday 20th March 2008: I hope this whole experience has shocked Daniel into realising the consequences of his behaviour – I don't want my son embarking on a life of crime.

I didn't think things could get any worse than they already were, but early the following week I heard two pieces of news. The first was that Daniel's exclusion had been made permanent. I had no quibble with that at all – I knew the school had done everything they could to support him over the two and a half years he'd been there, and I could see there was no other option this time.

The second bit of news was that the school had reported the incident to the police and he would have to go in for an interview.

And so, the following day, we went to our local police station for what I assumed would be 'a bit of a talking to'. In fact, it was an official – but voluntary – interview, and I was told that if I had refused to take Daniel in, he'd have been arrested, taken to a larger police station, fingerprinted and photographed. This was my ten-year-old son they were talking about.

Fortunately, we were both cooperative and Daniel was given the chance to put his side of the story across. Those 50 minutes in a police interview room were perhaps the most unsettling of my life. Daniel was frighteningly honest about what had happened and visibly shocked when the police officer told him that three people had been injured during his meltdown. One teacher had a bruised leg where she'd got in the way while Daniel was trying to kick the door; another had bruises on her knee from trying to hold the door shut; and a third had a sore wrist and bruised ribs and legs. It was a shock to me too and really brought home the severity of the situation. Suddenly, I could see a terrifying future for Daniel – one full of violence and crime and prison sentences.

Apparently, the school hadn't wanted to report the incident but had no option as staff had been injured, and once the police are involved, they have to take action. The scariest thing was that, at the age of ten, Daniel could have been formally charged with assault. The case was handed over to the Youth Offending Team and, after a home visit, they decided to give him an Informal Warning – the lowest course of action available to them.

On the way home from the police station, my heart broke in pieces as my small boy sobbed and sobbed.

Although he'd seemed to cope very well while we were there, the whole experience had really shaken him. I know his behaviour was inexcusable, but this was a horrible thing to go through for both of us, and I know it's something that has stayed in Daniel's mind ever since.

So here we were, four months past Daniel's tenth birthday and facing another school exclusion.

This time, though, it was completely justified and it seemed to have spurred on the local authority to do something. The county was lucky enough to have a special school that specialised in children with EBD – Emotional and Behavioural Difficulties – and they were sure it was the perfect place for Daniel. The only problem was he needed a Statement of Educational Needs to be given a place there, and the statementing process took months.

In the meantime, he was assigned a home tutor who came round every day for two hours to work with him. The tutor confidently told me that she'd found that other children with ADHD really benefited from this one-to-one attention, so Daniel was bound to thrive in the home-schooling environment.

How wrong could she be?

At first everything seemed to be going well. By that time I'd left my well-paid job and was running a small business from home; I'd also taken on a second job that meant I had to be in front of the computer all day, which meant Daniel was left to his own devices a lot of the time. By the time the tutor arrived, he had had enough of playing games or watching the TV and was ready for some work. But the novelty soon wore off and Daniel began to find being at home and isolated from his friends difficult to cope with. His response was – as always – to play up, and he started refusing to do any work, meaning the two-hour sessions became a drawn-out battle between him and the tutor to see who would cave in first.

The idea was they would read for the first part of the session, then complete some worksheets, then finish the lesson with some maths games on the computer. Daniel loved the maths games, and on a good day he'd read really quickly – without taking in any of the content – before scribbling his answers on the worksheet so he had the maximum time available on the computer. On bad days he just refused point-blank to do anything at all, saying it was stupid or boring or too easy.

One of Daniel's more endearing – and frustrating – characteristics is that he has a very logical view of the way the world works. On one occasion he refused every suggestion the tutor made until she said he could choose a book and read. So he chose a book and started reading to himself – but that wasn't what she wanted; she wanted him to read it out loud. After a logically fought discussion in which Daniel said that he didn't see the point of reading out loud, because he was much better and faster at reading in his head, he did read aloud – but in a silly voice. He had the book in his lap but the tutor asked him to put it on the table so she could see the words. After, quite logically, questioning why she needed to see the words when he was reading them out to her, he did move the book – but snapped when she started running her finger along each sentence as he read it. At this point he threw the book across the room, shouted,

'I hate you, you bloody woman, I never want to see you again,' and barricaded himself in his room.

I was horrified by his behaviour, but at the same time a part of me was on his side – after all, he wasn't stupid, he just had ADHD!

The only tutor Daniel ever really responded to was a guy who came round once a week to take him out for some exercise – usually to kick a football round a local park. Daniel really respected this tutor and had some frank conversations with him too. I was very sad when he left the education service to be a sports coach at a local football team – he was a very good influence on Daniel.

After several months of struggling to teach Daniel at home, the tutors decided that to continue was to endanger his mental health. He was bored, lonely, depressed and angry, and they didn't want to make things any worse for him. They put pressure on the local authority to hurry up with the statementing process so Daniel could go back into school in September and they retreated, leaving me with some work to do with Daniel in the few weeks before term ended. I'm no fan of home schooling – I firmly believe children are best educated in a school setting, alongside other children and with qualified teachers – but I did my best and, by making sure schoolwork was the first thing we did and TV and the PlayStation were only allowed when the work was complete, we struggled through to the summer holidays. But the months of isolation had taken their toll on my lovely little boy and he had lost his sparkle. He was a shadow of his former feisty funny self, and I wondered if the real Daniel would ever come back.

Support for Your Child in School

Monday 7th July 2008: Daniel's meant to be starting at special school soon, but getting him a Statement of Needs is taking so long. In the meantime, he's struggling with the home tutoring, he's lost his spark and I'm really worried about how he will cope when he eventually gets back into school. Please, can someone tell me when 2008 is going to get better?

When I wrote the first edition of this book back in 2013, the process and provision of special education needs was going through big changes. At that time Daniel had been on the School Action and School Action Plus levels of support and was later assessed for a Statement of Educational Needs. Since September 2014 the system has changed massively, with School Action/Action Plus becoming SEN Support, and Statements phased out and replaced with Education, Health and Care Plans – EHCPs. If your child already has a Statement, they will be transferred to the new ECHP at the next transition period – usually at the end of Key Stage 1 or 2. If you're applying for the first time, then your child will automatically be assessed for an EHCP.

A bit later in this chapter I'll talk about our experience of applying for a Statement of Needs, but, first, here's some information on the new system.

SEN Support

Until recently there were two levels of SEN Support in schools – one that relied on the school's internal resources and one that enabled the school to call on external help. Both levels are now covered by SEN Support, which is available for any child who has special educational needs to help them achieve in school.

Part of the old system involved IEPs – Individual Education Plans – which detailed the targets set for the child, the support put in place and the end result. IEPs have now been abolished, although many schools still use them, but any child with additional needs who gets SEN Support must have a detailed SEN record kept about them. The report needs to include:

- what special educational needs have been identified

- what outcomes the school expects the child to achieve with SEN provision

- what provision has been put in place.

The school – usually class teacher and SENCO – and parents should meet up regularly – at least three times a year – to update the SEN record using an assess–plan–do–review process. If it's found that the school can't provide enough additional help for the child to achieve the outcomes, then either the school or the parent can request an assessment for the next stage of support – an Education, Health and Care Plan.

Education, Health and Care Plan

Getting an assessment for additional help for a child who is clearly struggling in school should be a straightforward process, but, as with anything that involves the government's money, it tends to be anything but. My experience of applying for a Statement was that it was a long, drawn-out, painful and frustrating process. Back then the parent was the only person who could request an assessment – even though the school would have been more likely to know the limits of any support they were offering – and it took months for all the relevant evidence to be gathered and collated and reviewed before the Statement was actually issued. The timescales for an Education, Health and Care Plan are slightly shorter, but it still takes a long time and involves lots of paperwork.

If you feel your child's needs are not being met by SEN Support, you can apply to your local authority for an assessment for an Education, Health and Care Plan. The school, doctor, health visitor and even the child or young person themselves can also request an assessment. The plans are available for anyone up to the age of 25 who is in full time education – this is to reflect that fact that many young people with disabilities need longer to complete their formal education, and that support shouldn't stop at 16, as it did with the statementing system. However, EHCPs are only statutory up to A Levels or equivalent qualifications and apprenticeships; although they can be used as guidance for support needed by those students who go on to higher education, there is no legal requirement for universities to implement the support.

While the old Statement of Educational Needs looked at what support a child needed to help them achieve academically, the new Education, Health and Care Plan takes into account the wishes, views and feelings of the child and their family and is focused on the outcomes they want to achieve both now and in the future. This means the EHCP is much more tailored to the needs of each individual child. For example, rather than focusing on the child achieving on a level with their peers, the outcomes of the EHCP might look at what support is needed to enable the child to leave school with some qualifications, participate in the community, gain employment and, ultimately, live independently.

While education – the E in EHCP – is obviously very important, the plan pulls together health and social care as well, ensuring that a child with disabilities is supported more holistically. For example, many children with ADHD also have autistic spectrum disorders, anxiety or Dyspraxia. The plan outlines all the support the child needs to achieve the desired outcomes, so that could include speech therapy, counselling or occupational therapy. Social care is also included, meaning there may be extra support for out-of-school activities such as sports, or respite care for carers. The final version of the ECHP also names the school that's considered the best placement for the child.

To being the process of getting an Education, Health and Care Plan you need to prove that your child is not achieving their full potential in their current educational setting – and that can be difficult. There's a very good blog site called Special Needs Jungle, which I've included details of in Appendix 3. Their advice is to arm yourself with as much knowledge and information as you can to support your application, because, without that, it's very easy for the authorities to brush you aside.

First, you need to be fully aware of what your child is achieving and the difficulties they are experiencing in their current school. Talk to the SENCO (Special Educational Needs Co-ordinator) at your child's school, ask to see their SEN Support record, and ask the teachers how they feel your child is coping. If the school has concerns that your child is under-achieving because they can't provide enough support for their needs, contact your local authority education department and request an assessment for an Education, Health and Care Plan, or ask the school to apply for one.

Having a medical diagnosis of a condition is a bonus in the assessment game because it's much harder to ignore than if a parent just has a hunch about their child. If your child hasn't been formally diagnosed with ADHD, ask your GP for a referral to a paediatrician for an assessment. Yes, it's not nice giving your child a label but it can make all the difference when it comes to getting additional help. If you receive any reports or assessments from medical professionals, keep them safe as you may need them as evidence of your child's disability. Tell your child's doctor/paediatrician/psychiatrist that you are applying for an EHCP assessment, because their support could be crucial.

It's worth researching your local authority and finding out what their education policies are, because if you can prove that they don't meet your child's needs, or that your child is not achieving goals mentioned in the policies, you're halfway there. You need to present a strong case for your child to be awarded an EHCP, so keep notes and include absolutely every little bit of evidence in your application. Filling in the paperwork can be daunting, but there is a lot of help available online and organisations such as SOS SEN and IPSEA (details in Appendix 3) will help you complete it.

Once you've requested an assessment, the local authority has six weeks to decide whether or not to do one. If they agree, they'll then collect reports from your child's school and request assessments from medical practitioners such as your child's doctor or CAMHS consultant, and they'll also ask you to submit a report on what your child's needs are and what outcomes you want them to achieve.

Once the local authority has received all the information they need, they'll put together a draft plan, and you have 15 days to comment on the plan and decide on a named school. Then the plan will be finalised and the support (hopefully) put in place. The entire process can take up to 20 weeks from the date of the initial assessment to the production of the final Education, Health and Care Plan.

If you're not happy about any part of the process – the decision not to assess, not to give an EHCP, the support in the plan or the named school – you can appeal, first directly with the local authority, and then via SENDIST.

There are two other additions to the SEN process – a Personal Budget, which gives parents more control over where support comes from, and the Local Offer, which outlines all the services and support available in your area.

Personal Budgets and Direct Payments

When you apply for an Education, Health and Care Plan for your child, you can also request a Personal Budget – a breakdown of the notional costs of each element of support – and Direct Payments. This gives you more control over who provides the support outlined in the plan – for example, you may prefer to choose your own speech therapist or counsellor rather than use the one the local authority supplies. There are only two occasions when you can request a Personal Budget and Direct Payments – during the initial assessment or review of the EHCP – and there's no guarantee your request will be accepted.

Local Offer

Since September 2014 all local authorities, by law, have to show the services and support available from them for children and young people with disabilities and special educational needs. This Local Offer is likely to include: what support is available through schools and colleges in the area for children with disabilities or special educational needs; education, health and care provision; training provision; transport to and from school; and support for young adults to make the transition to independent living.

You should be able to find your local authority's Local Offer by searching online or visiting their website. Every area offers different things, but as an example, as well as covering the basics of education, social and health care provision, my area's Local Offer includes information on mental health services, disability sports programmes, youth services and respite care.

⟨───◆───⟩

Back to the story... In our case, the LEA was initially going to place Daniel in another mainstream school, but on advice from his previous head teacher and his home tutors it was decided that the local EBD (Emotional and Behavioural Difficulties) special school would actually be the right setting for him. However, he would only be offered a place there if he had a Statement naming the school, so the LEA had no choice but to start the process.

In some ways the idea of a special school sent shudders through me – although every child is special, it's difficult to admit that your child is 'special' and not able to cope in mainstream school. At the same time I knew this was going to give Daniel the best chance of success – and what other option did we have? My biggest fear was that a return to mainstream school would end with a third permanent exclusion, and I didn't know if either Daniel or I would survive that.

As well as naming a school, the Statement included the recommendations of a host of medical and educational professionals, so the next few months meant seemingly endless assessments for Daniel with the educational psychologist, our CAMHS paediatrician, another doctor from the local children's hospital and a clinical psychiatrist. There were also reports from Daniel's former school, his tutors and the Behaviour Support team. I was asked to submit information on why I felt Daniel should be given a Statement of Needs – never one to pass up on the opportunity to share my views, I wrote a long essay outlining Daniel's behaviour over the years and why I felt he deserved a third chance.

It took three months for the provisional Statement to be compiled, which I then had to approve before the process could move on. Following that, the named school had 15 days to come to a decision on whether they would offer Daniel a place – although my understanding is that once a school has been named on a Statement, they have to have a very good reason not to accept that child. So I thought it would be a matter of days before Daniel would have a school place and that perhaps he'd even be able to attend for a few weeks towards the end of the summer term.

Typically, that didn't happen. The school was concerned because, at the age of ten, Daniel would be going into Year 6 in September and they normally preferred to take children in a year or two before that.

They were unsure that they would have enough time to work with him before he'd be leaving again for senior school. This meant that, rather than just making a snap decision, Daniel's case would be taken to a 'Four Heads' review, where the heads of the four special schools in the county would discuss his situation. Then it was decided that as there were a few children heading for Year 6, they would hold an extra-ordinary meeting to resolve their cases in one go. This all meant that the decision was delayed way beyond the fifteenth day and there was no way he would be back in school before September – if he was even given a place at all. There was still no guarantee of that.

But finally, on 17th July 2008 I received the phone call I'd been waiting for. Daniel had been offered a place in the special EBD school and, following an admission meeting early in September, he'd be back in full-time education. September couldn't come soon enough.

Disability Living Allowance and Other Benefits

While the statementing process was going on, our paediatrician at CAMHS suggested that we apply for DLA – Disability Living Allowance. It wasn't something I'd ever thought about before – after all, Daniel had ADHD, but in my eyes he wasn't disabled – but the paediatrician said he would support us in our application. I thought the money would come in handy for organising some family treats – everything had to be very carefully planned with Daniel – and replacing some of the toys and household objects he'd broken in his meltdowns, so we went ahead.

From April 2013 the government started phasing out DLA for those aged 16–24 and replacing it with PIP – Personal Independence Payments. Anyone over the age of 16 applying for the first time will apply for PIP, although, at the time of writing, children under the age of 16 can still apply for DLA, and those already receiving the benefit will continue to get it till their sixteenth birthday, after which time they will be transferred on to PIP, depending on where they live. See Appendix 2 for useful links on DLA and PIP, including how to find out when a child over 16 will be transferred to the new benefit.

The DLA form is huge and takes hours to complete. It's also one of the most emotionally depressing tasks I've ever had to do. When you have a child with special needs, you take your victories wherever you can – you have to, otherwise you just wouldn't be able to cope with everyday life. You praise every tiny thing they do right; you see success in the smallest achievements and you cherish that.

The DLA application turns on its head everything you try to do as a parent, because you have to look at your child in as negative a way as possible. The allowance is awarded (if you're lucky) if you can demonstrate that, because of their disability, your child needs significantly more or different care and support than a neurotypical child of their age. To do that, you have to view every aspect of their life at its worst, and pick up on all the deficiencies and difficulties. And when you're probably feeling like you've been through the emotional wringer a few times already, that can be really hard to do – but if you paint a picture that's as rosy as you like to imagine life is, you won't stand a chance of getting the allowance.

When the form arrived, I felt a bit daunted by it but I did some research online and found lots of help on how to fill it in – try searching for 'DLA ADHD' or 'DLA autism' for help, as the advice is relevant across both conditions. Depending on where you live, there may also be a local organisation that can help you with your application. Contact a Family (www.cafamily.org. uk) has a free helpline you can call to find out about local support in your area. I've also included some tips in Appendix 2.

The DLA form covers several aspects of daily life and you need to focus on the areas where your child needs additional help and support. For example, until fairly recently Daniel was completely disorganised, especially in the mornings, so I would need to place his clothes out ready for school, and then prompt him to get dressed because he'd get halfway through and then get distracted. At mealtimes the same thing could happen – he'd get distracted and stop eating and would need reminding. When we were out and about, he needed constant monitoring because although he has a good sense of road safety, he could become easily distracted and wander off. And, of course, there was always the chance that someone would wind him up and he'd flip and have a meltdown. Nowadays he's started to become more independent but he still needs additional support with things like finding his way around, managing money and completing paperwork, he can need reminding about personal hygiene issues and he needs motivating to do basic everyday tasks.

All these are practical examples of how Daniel needs care over and above that needed by a neurotypical child of his age. In reality, though, everything I've ever done for Daniel has just been what I needed to do and I've never viewed it as being anything different; it was just the way it was. As parents, it's easy to view the support you give as being 'normal' – but when you're completing the DLA form, you need to look closely at what additional support you give your child over other children their age, and include everything!

If you are thinking about putting in a claim for DLA, I've included a couple of useful websites in the Resources section (Appendix 3). They'll help you understand what the assessors look for and how you can work out what extra help your child needs – even if these are things you just accept as part of everyday life.

In some cases children need to go through a medical assessment before a decision about DLA is made, but we were fortunate and the application, along with supporting references from our CAMHS paediatrician, was enough and DLA was awarded. In my heart, I still don't consider Daniel to be a child with a disability – and in many ways he appears to be a 'normal' teenager now, although he does still have issues – but I have been very grateful for the little bit of money we receive each month.

Additional benefits

Once your child has a diagnosis, or if they receive Disability Living Allowance, there is other support you can access. What's available often depends on your personal circumstances or where you live.

If you receive Child Tax Credits and your child is awarded DLA, you can claim additional money and, depending on the severity of your child's condition and the number of hours you care for them, you may be eligible for Carer's Allowance.

Each local authority also has its own support services for disabled children and their families. For example, where I live there are holiday playschemes, day and short-break respite care, youth groups and disability sports programmes.

There's even a national cinema scheme where carers get free admission – you can apply at www.ceacard.co.uk – and many of the big tourist attractions will give you preferential treatment, such as allowing you into the fast-track queues, if you can prove your child has a disability that makes waiting problematic. Have a squirrel around their website FAQs to see if they offer any help for people with additional needs and disabilities.

The easiest way to find out what's available to you is to check out the website of the Information, Advice and Support Services Network, which used to be known as Parent Partnership (IASSnetwork.org.uk). They'll be able to direct you to local organisations that can offer you advice and support on benefits and more.

Special School

Thursday 11th September 2008: I just don't understand Daniel. For eight months now he's been out of school and desperate to go back. He's been bored and lonely and hasn't responded well to the home tuition because really all he wanted was to be a normal kid in a normal class with other normal kids. Well, today he gets that chance. We're off to visit his new school (OK, it's a special school rather than a 'normal' mainstream one, but it's for kids like him) and he's being such a pain about it. He won't wash his face, he won't clean his teeth and he got himself dressed into the most awful filthy t-shirt imaginable, and then made a huge fuss about wearing a clean one. I explained that if he went looking like that they'd take one look at him and say they didn't want him in school – and that this was his only chance because the only other option would be a special boarding school.

'That's OK,' he says. 'At least there might be something to keep me entertained there. Better than being here with you.'

Ouch, that hurt. But after eight months of being at home with me, isolated from children his own age, I could understand how he felt – and why he was using his usual avoidance tactic to delay the visit to his new school. He was scared and apprehensive, and he didn't know what to expect. Fortunately, though, I managed to get him dressed and in the car and at the new school – and it's been the absolute making of him.

For the last six years of his formal education, Daniel attended special schools – first a primary, then a senior school – and they had an incredible effect on him. Both schools have an ethos based around reward and consequences, and children with ADHD really respond well to this system. Everything good the children do, whether academic or behavioural, is rewarded.

At the primary school, children received points that they could trade in for various small toys and treats each week, or save for bigger things. The senior school also awarded points, with each point representing a penny. The boys could earn up to £5 a week for good behaviour, effort in class, wearing the correct uniform and so on. The points could be carried over or used for treats or extra school trips, but if they misbehaved, they paid for their behaviour through their points – even a broken pencil meant losing the equivalent of 50p. When they leave school, the students are presented with a cheque for the balance of their points, and some boys leave school with several hundred pounds to set them up in adult life. Both reward schemes proved popular with Daniel and, better still, he responded well to them – and that spurred him on towards improved behaviour and academic success.

Both the schools he attended are aimed at kids who have failed in – or perhaps been let down by – mainstream education. These children arrive at the special school angry with the world and themselves and low in confidence. The lessons are set up with success as the main priority. Learning is done in small, manageable blocks with rewards for each achievement, however minor. Bad behaviour is dealt with firmly. The head teacher told me they rarely exclude – exclusion is all these kids have known in the past, so they often deliberately test the system to its limits, and it could be the last chance they have – but the discipline is tough but fair, with detentions and withdrawn privileges keeping most children on the right track.

Daniel settled into his new school quickly and after so many months at home he was ready and waiting for the taxi every morning. (As he had a Statement, and the school was 20 miles from our home, the local authority provided transport.) He came home each night with a small piece of homework – no more than ten minutes – and mostly he did it without hesitation. His teacher really seemed to get on well with him and it was lovely to receive regular phone calls, not to tell me he was having a meltdown and needed collecting, but to let me know he was having a good day and was 'a pleasure to teach'!

He spent the whole of Year 6 at the primary EBD – Emotional and Behavioural Difficulties – special school and, apart from the odd blip here and there, he did incredibly well. Despite my best efforts and the best efforts of the home tutors, he had fallen behind academically because of the time he spent at home, but he quickly caught up once he was back in full-time school and he started to enjoy the lessons too. Handwriting has always been an issue for him, but in a setting where the teachers were fully aware of his problems and had techniques and tools specially designed for children like Daniel, he was soon writing whole pages of stories – something I never expected him to do!

The following September he moved to the linked senior school – again a specialist EBD school – and he continued to thrive there. My first visit to the school filled me with apprehension; there were locks on the doors and the whole place felt a bit like a prison. Then I thought about it sensibly. Daniel was only 11 at the time, but I knew how angry and aggressive and violent he could be when he had a meltdown – imagine a boy of 16 acting that way! The locks were in place to protect the boys and the staff, and although the school looked a bit shabby and run down, it was actually something of a haven, with staff who were wonderful and caring, staff who want the boys to succeed in school – and in life. There was also an on-site policeman – again, a fact that seemed a bit scary at first, but he became a good friend to many of the boys and it was beneficial for them to be able to get to know an authority figure in a safe space.

Daniel has always been bright – he was on the Able Child register as well as the Special Needs one from an early age – and I was concerned that although special school would help him with his behavioural needs, it wouldn't stretch him enough academically. However, the fact that he was in a class of 6–8, with a teacher and a teaching assistant, worked in his favour, and in most subjects he was able to work at his own level. The school kept in close contact with me throughout Daniel's time there, and if there were problems, they would ring me to let me know what was going on, which I appreciated – although it didn't happen often. One day Daniel got into a fight with a boy and ended up with a broken hand, and there were a few other hiccups here and there, but overall he did very well in special school.

Because of the nature of the school, academic success was sometimes difficult to achieve, so the school set out to give the boys plenty of experiences to show them just what life has to offer. Remember, these are boys who have been rejected, often more than once, by mainstream education, and they often arrive feeling there's no point in them doing anything because the world is already out to get them. During the five years Daniel was at the school, he tried deep sea fishing, rock climbing and go-karting; he went on trips to Wales and Barcelona; and he had the opportunity to try photography, gardening, cooking, aromatherapy and meditation. End-of-term treats included bowling, cinema and theme parks, and he also took part in the finals of a national first aid competition and learned to play the drums. All these experiences helped him realise that life did have something to offer him, and that he could achieve anything with the right support.

However, he did still have difficulties – and one of his biggest challenges came with art class. Because the school was so small – around 70 boys – they didn't have the teaching staff available to offer options at GCSE level, so the boys did whatever subjects were available. That meant Daniel – who hates art, has never seen the point of art – had to do GCSE Art. Big problem! At the start of Year 10 his teacher called to say she knew how much he hated it, but he was disrupting the rest of the class – could I think of anything vaguely art-related he could do to keep him occupied while she got on with teaching those who did want to learn? We decided he could do his own project on computer games graphics – he's always been a big computer games player – and he seemed enthusiastic about the idea. I was really thankful that the school were willing and able to be so flexible in their approach to learning, rather than just forcing Daniel to do something he quite obviously hated.

Interestingly, he actually decided the project was 'too much like hard work' and decided to do the course work instead. With some help from a teaching assistant, he discovered that when he puts his mind to it he can actually draw and paint quite well – and guess what? He really enjoyed art lessons from then on. It seems the whole 'I hate art, it's boring' resistance was just another avoidance tactic because he didn't have the confidence to have a go in case he failed.

With GCSEs looming, the school began to prepare the pupils well in advance, and in summer 2012 Daniel sat exams in English, maths, science and PE. Considering he was in a special school and taking exams a year early, we were delighted when he got C in English and maths and D in science and PE! The idea was he'd take more exams at the end of Year 11, and retake science to try to get a higher grade. The future was looking very positive.

But then disaster struck, with two huge losses for Daniel within the space of a week. First, he found out that his favourite teaching assistant was leaving the school. He'd become very attached to this particular person and the news was devastating. But, to make matters worse, four days later Daniel's father died very suddenly, after a short illness. He and I had been separated for a long time, and Daniel and his sister had not seen their dad much over the last two years, but, even so, it was a terrible shock and we all struggled to cope. Over the next few months Katie went through the normal grief cycle of shock, denial, anger, depression and acceptance. Daniel, on the other hand, was already too consumed with the loss of his teacher to even begin to cope with anything else. And I struggled to support them both, while dealing with a confusing mix of emotions myself.

Daniel returned to school in September and seemed to be managing, but very soon it became apparent that he was deeply disturbed. There were many angry outbursts, lots of defiance and some quite worrying depressive moments. One day he told a teacher that his life was so bad he might as well kill himself... I received a panicky phone call from the school and an emergency appointment was set up with CAMHS, who offered him anti-depressants, which he turned down.

While we were there, the paediatrician suddenly reached for a folder, brought out a sheet of paper, ticked off lots of boxes and announced that she thought Daniel had Asperger's Syndrome as well as ADHD! Actually, it wasn't as much of a surprise to me as it could have been. His original diagnosis had been for ADHD, ODD and autistic traits, but as the hyperactivity and defiance tailed off as he got older, I was becoming more and more aware of his quirky nature, lack of creativity, literal interpretations and social awkwardness. I'd always thought that people with Asperger's avoided eye contact, whereas Daniel maintains eye contact perhaps a little too intensely – but apparently that can be a sign too! This new diagnosis made a lot of sense to me.

It made sense to the SENCO at the school too, who had been struggling to manage Daniel's behaviour with traditional ADHD strategies, and she began to implement some new techniques. The school also arranged for a counsellor who specialised in children on the autistic spectrum to work with Daniel on a regular basis, and this really helped him to begin to come to terms with his grief and get back on track.

By June 2014 Daniel was emerging from the darkness of depression and ready to face the rest of his GCSE exams – although he did very little revision and had a 'what will be, will be' attitude! As a result he didn't improve on his results of the year before – but he did secure enough grades to get a place at a local college to take a BTEC IT course.

So despite the difficulties of the last year, it seemed my fears about special school were unfounded. Far from struggling academically, Daniel came on in leaps and bounds, and I just know that if he had gone back into a mainstream school, his education would have continued to be disrupted. Although at first I felt awkward telling people where he went – there's a certain stigma about your child being at special school – I now tell them with pride, because I know he was in exactly the right educational environment. I'm so pleased we found a school that worked for Daniel, where he felt valued and accepted. If you're ever faced with the decision of whether to give special school a shot, my advice would be to go for it – if the local authority feels it's the best environment for your child, they're probably right.

Tips and Techniques for Dealing with ADHD

Over the years Daniel has given me a wide range of challenges to deal with, from verbal abuse and defiance to aggression, violence and meltdowns. Fortunately, we are at a stage now where the combination of medication, the right school and an increasing maturity has brought Daniel's behaviour under control. However, there are many tips, tricks and techniques I've tried over the years that have made a difference. Not all of the following will be relevant or appropriate for your child, but I hope you'll find something here that you can use to good effect.

Choose your battles carefully
When you have a child with ADHD, it can seem that your entire day is spent reprimanding them. If you punished your child for every single bit of bad behaviour, they'd probably spend most of their life in Time Out!

I've learned over the years to pick my battles carefully – for example, although I've never been happy with Daniel using bad language at home, it's the lesser of many evils compared with some of the other behaviours he's shown. I've learned that it's best to ignore some things, in some situations, as long as no damage is being done to people or property; and Daniel knows that although he can get away with swearing at home, it's not acceptable in other settings. That way he can use the pressure valve of the odd swear word here and there at home, which seems to help him manage his behaviour better overall.

Routine

A firm routine is one of the most important things you can put in place to help your ADHD child. In my experience, kids like these don't cope well with change and are at their best when they know what to expect, so having set times for daily events is essential. I know some parents have the day's routine written on a poster on the wall; I never tried that, but we did try to stick to the same dinner, bath and bed times every night. It wasn't always easy, and often Daniel's behaviour would affect our routine adversely, but I'm sure it made a difference. Even now, at 18, he is a man of habit who does many of the same things at the same times every day.

Consistency and 'following through'

Following on from routine, you need to be as consistent as possible in managing your child's behaviour. Set the rules, make sure your child knows what kind of behaviour is and isn't acceptable, and be consistent. Don't punish your child for something one day that you let them get away with another time – they will just become even more confused about how they should behave, which will lead to more frustration and more bad behaviour. As with your daily routine, you might find it useful to list the unacceptable behaviours on a poster on the wall – for example, we do not hit people, we do not swear, we do not kick – so your child knows exactly what's what. If you give consequences for bad behaviour, then make sure you are prepared to enforce them. Once or twice I threatened Daniel with missing out on a treat if he didn't behave, but because I didn't want his sister to miss out too he still got to do whatever it was, which meant next time I threatened something he didn't believe it would ever happen and just carried on misbehaving!

Reverse reward charts

I never found that the traditional sticker-type reward charts worked with Daniel. I think he found it hard to visualise the chart full of stickers or the resulting reward, so he didn't see the point of trying to get the stickers in the first place. What we found did work was a kind of reverse reward system. I filled a jar with objects – we used the glass beads used for flower arrangements, but it could be coins, tokens, Lego pieces, anything really – and every time Daniel misbehaved and broke the rules in some way he lost a bead. At the end of the week any beads left in the jar were converted into pocket money or sweet money.

Somehow, being able to see the starting total and watch it decrease seemed to be more effective than trying to add to a chart. Of course, you need to make sure the rules are very clear to your child in advance so they know what is and isn't acceptable. If your child is really struggling to behave well, start small – give them just one or two things that they need to stop doing, rather than a whole list of rules and regulations, and add more as you go.

Ignore silly behaviours

Many ADHD behaviours are annoying more than anything, and often the best way to deal with them is to ignore them completely. Sometimes Daniel would act in a really silly way, maybe talking in a baby voice, banging toys together or fidgeting around, and the more attention I gave him – through asking him to stop, telling him off and so on – the more he would do it. I decided that as long as the behaviour wasn't dangerous – to Daniel, other people or property – the best way to deal with it was to ignore him. Once I stopped paying him any attention, he often got bored and stopped the silly behaviour. Even now Daniel occasionally has a silly half hour, and although his face pulling or dancing around can be annoying to other people, we have learned to ignore it.

Restraint, removal and distraction during meltdowns

The best thing I've found to do when Daniel gets angry or has a meltdown is leave him to calm down, because the more people try to help him, the more out of control and angry he gets. Often just backing away and giving him space is enough to avoid a complete meltdown. However, it's not always possible to leave a child alone to calm themselves, either because the location is not safe or there are other people around who could get hurt. In these cases, do whatever you can to remove your child to a place of safety or, if that's not possible, just try to keep people away as much as you can. When Daniel was small, if I could, I would sit on the floor with him on my lap and hold him firmly till he was more calm, all the time talking to him in a soft voice. I think often when children have meltdowns they scare themselves with the intensity of their anger, which makes them even more defensive and aggressive, so giving them reassurance that they will be OK and will not come to any harm seems to help.

If you can, learn the signs that your child is heading for a meltdown and try to deflect it. When Daniel is getting stressed, his whole body tenses up, his mouth becomes a tight line and I can see him start to shake. At this stage I try to find some way of changing what's going on to see if we can avoid an explosion. It doesn't always work, but distraction can be very effective in the right circumstances.

For example, on one occasion my nanna, who was in her nineties, kept poking Daniel in the side and telling him what a lovely boy he was, which for some reason really annoyed him. I could see he was close to exploding. I mentioned that both the children had started going to dance classes and they decided to give an impromptu demonstration. By the time they finished, Daniel had forgotten he was feeling angry earlier – meltdown deflected!

Giving praise

Giving praise has so many benefits. Apart from helping a child's self-esteem, it shows them the difference between good and bad behaviour, and helps to set boundaries and rules. On a bad day with a child with ADHD, it can often be difficult to see anything to give praise for, but I believe strongly in finding something – anything – no matter how small. In the past I've praised Daniel for *not* breaking a toy, for sitting still for five minutes and for eating his dinner. You probably wouldn't see those as worthy of praise in your average kid, but it made a huge difference in our lives, and giving praise made me feel better too!

Praise your child for everything that goes right, however small. Be specific with your praise – don't just say 'Well done' or 'That was good.' Point out exactly what it was that went well. Better still, let your child know how their behaviour made you feel. For example: 'Thank you for putting your dirty clothes in the washing basket. It makes me feel really happy when I don't have so much work to do.' When your child misbehaves, always make it clear that it is the behaviour you are angry or disappointed about, not the child.

Be patient, and don't hold grudges

Patience often feels like it's in short supply when you're dealing with a child with ADHD, but patience is also one of your key tools. ADHD behaviours can push you to breaking point, but losing your temper is not going to make things any better. Try to understand that there is nearly always a reason why your child is behaving badly; you may not be able to see the trigger or understand how important it is to your child, but just knowing that there is one makes a big difference. Once you begin to understand that your child isn't misbehaving deliberately but is responding to something that's upset them – however silly that thing might be – it's easier to deal with the outcome. Being patient with your child and keeping your cool, however far they push you, helps your child calm down more quickly than if you shout and yell at them. Also remember that your child will probably forget both the trigger and the resulting behaviour almost straight away. Once they're calm, ask them for an apology, accept it graciously, deliver any consequences straight away and then let it go. Each day is a new one, so don't linger on your child's past behaviour, however bad it may have been at the time.

The distraction method

When a child gets into a loop of disruptive or defiant behaviour, sometimes all it takes is something to distract them momentarily, because that gives their brain the chance to switch from one pattern to another, resulting in the end of a stalemate situation. Try changing the subject completely, agreeing with the child or throwing something completely random into the conversation. I've found that when Daniel gets into an 'I don't care' conversation, sometimes just saying 'Well, I do care' stops him in his tracks. I've also found that throwing something really random into the conversation can help. On a couple of occasions when Daniel was having a tantrum, I threw one of my own. The shock of seeing his mother acting in such a silly way – lying on the floor, screaming and thumping the ground – was enough to make him realise how silly his own behaviour was, and he immediately stopped stropping and laughed at me instead. Of course, I wouldn't recommend trying this technique in the supermarket!

Sport and other energetic activities

Most children with ADHD have bundles of energy and it can help to give them a safe arena in which to unleash that energy. Sport is an excellent way of doing this, and team sports can be especially effective for ADHD children, who often see the world in black and white and have a strong regard for the rules of a game. Daniel has always enjoyed playing football and although he struggled with casual games at school lunchtimes when the rules of the game weren't enforced fully – for example, after someone scored the ball might be played from the goal mouth rather than the centre circle – he was much better able to cope within a team, where the game was played 'properly'. Individual activities such as trampolining, martial arts, dance and swimming are also a good way to let them use up all that excess energy!

Dealing with inflexibility

Family life with a child who is inflexible can be difficult to manage, because every time you want to do something you run the risk of refusal or even a meltdown from your child. I found that giving a countdown made a huge difference to how Daniel managed change. For example, if we were visiting a friend for the afternoon, I would tell Daniel that we'd be leaving in three hours, then keep him updated throughout the morning that we would leave in two hours, one hour and so on, down to ten minutes, five minutes, two minutes… This way he had time to switch his brain from one activity to another, and by the time we actually left the house he was much more willing to cooperate. Then I'd do the same at the friend's house, to prepare him for coming home again! Of course, doing this means it's difficult to do spontaneous activities, but life was much easier for the whole family when Daniel was able to join in without becoming distressed.

Offering choices

Children with ADHD often feel that because their behaviour is out of their control, they need to take control in other areas of life to compensate and that can cause big problems. By offering your child options (but making sure you choose what those options are) you can give them the feeling that they are in control, while limiting the outcome. For example, you can offer three different dinners, let them choose an activity from one of two or give them an either/or decision.

This can even work in terms of consequences for their actions too. Instead of telling them to go to their room – which is likely to end in a battle of wills – let them choose whether they go to their room or help you with the cleaning/lose the PlayStation for a day/ get less pocket money. (Just offer two options – but only you know what is most likely to be effective with your child.) Your child is more likely to accept the punishment without a fuss when they actually have some control over what it is.

Dealing with forgetfulness and lack of concentration

It can be really frustrating when a child with ADHD doesn't seem able to follow instructions or remember what to do. These are some of the techniques I've found that work for us:

1. Get down on their level and make sure they are looking at you as you speak to them. Often children look as if they are paying attention but their mind is actually elsewhere.

2. Be very specific and clear when you tell your child to do something. Don't leave anything to chance.

3. Keep lists very short – if possible, only ask them to do or remember one thing at a time.

4. Break tasks down into small manageable chunks. For example, don't just ask a child to tidy their bedroom; ask them to pick up the clothes, then when they've done that ask them to put them in the washing basket. Then ask them to put the books on the shelf, put toys in the box and so on – just one task at a time. Make each task very specific and then give praise for each task when it's complete.

Have serious chats in the car

One of the most frustrating things I've found about parenting Daniel is that he's often reluctant to talk to me when things have gone wrong. Many a time we've sat down on the sofa or at the table for a 'serious conversation' which has resulted in him refusing to talk to me, being silly, leaving the room or getting angry – so I often avoided having the conversation in the first place rather than risk yet another meltdown. However, we have had some very insightful conversations in the car. Of course, it's not always ideal, and it's something that has been more effective as Daniel has grown up, but being in an enclosed space where he can't escape and where, more importantly, I can't look him in the eye (without crashing the car!) seems to give him the opportunity to get things off his chest. Some of our most sensible discussions have happened on the way home from the paediatrician's or a school event. I used to dread long car journeys with the kids but now I look forward to them as we always have a good natter!

'Time Out' cards or code words

Daniel's junior school introduced me to the concept of 'Time Out' cards and it's a useful method that can be as effective at home as at school. It involves your child having a card they show you when they're getting stressed. Often children get so angry inside they can't express their feelings verbally, but showing the card lets you know what their mood is and you can then use other tactics – for example, giving them space to calm down – to help avoid a meltdown. Alternatively, give your child a specific word that they can use to warn you they are getting close to exploding. Of course, sometimes Daniel abused this tool if he just wanted to be left alone, but it has worked well for us and allowed him some control when he most needed it.

A note about traditional Time Out

I've read dozens of parenting books over the years and Time Out is a concept that I can see the point of but have always struggled with. The problem with Daniel was getting him to stay in the place where Time Out happened. We tried the bottom step, but after endlessly putting him back after he wandered away we often both got so stressed out that it induced a meltdown (and not just in Daniel!), making things ten times worse. Time Out normally happened in his room, and I have to admit at one stage when he was younger I resorted to tying a rope from the door handle to the banister to stop him coming out of his room – not something I'd recommend, though! Time Out in his room often meant he would trash the place, which was upsetting when toys were broken as a result, but it was a consequence for him to learn from.

Using timers

Kids with ADHD often don't have a very good understanding of time. When you tell them you're going out in an hour, they can't work out how long that is and will often nag at you to go early! Some parents find it useful to set a timer, so the child can physically see how long is left. You can also use timers for tasks like tidying the bedroom or doing homework – for example, giving the child ten minutes to pick up all their books before the buzzer goes off and offering a small reward if they do the task. Even more fun when it comes to bedroom tidying is to have a 'tidy song' – a favourite piece of music that you play at the end of every day while you all tidy away the toys!

You can also use timers in conjunction with Time Out, allowing the child out of their room when the timer goes off. For some reason, using a timer deflects some of the child's anger away from the parent, making Time Out easier for everyone.

As I said, these are some of the things that I've tried with Daniel, and they might not all work for you. I've asked other parents what techniques they use to manage their ADHD children and the following is one of the best ideas I heard:

The smiling technique

One of the best pieces of advice I was given was to smile when you catch your child looking at you. It's easy to get into the habit of being tired, cross, fed-up, etc. and if you look miserable your child will be too. The first day I tried it, I swear I thought my cheek muscles were on fire, they were so sore, and the kids thought I should be shipped off to the funny farm for leering at them every time they moved, but it does work. If someone smiles at you, you automatically smile back.

I haven't tried the smiling trick myself but I can see how it would work!

If you have any tried and tested techniques that have worked with your ADHD child, I'd love to hear about them. You can email me at alison@adhdkids.org.uk and I'll include your ideas in the next edition of this book!

ADHD from a Parent's Perspective

Being a parent is the most difficult job going, and when your child has special needs, it becomes even more challenging. Of course, as a mum I have made a promise of unconditional love to both my children – but Daniel has sorely tested that promise many times! OK, maybe that's going a little far, but I have to admit there has been the odd occasion when I wished I wasn't his mum or when I wished him away, and I've often despaired for his future. He's embarrassed me more times than I can count, he's hurt me both physically and emotionally, and the fight to get him the educational support he needed was a long and difficult struggle. Yet he's my boy and I love him – and his sister, Katie – more than anything.

Many people have asked me how I coped with Daniel's ADHD, how I managed to continue living a fairly normal life despite everything that was going on, and my answer is that I don't really know! Any parent of a child with special needs knows that you just get on with it. The stresses and strains are all you know, they're just part of life, and you knuckle down and deal with whatever is thrown at you – sometimes quite literally! I've had the support and help of my mum and a few close friends, who have all provided a listening ear, a hug and a shoulder to cry on many times, as well as giving me practical support too. I have a couple of friends who also have sons with ADHD and/or autism and they have been fantastically supportive. Just knowing you're not the only person going through all this makes a tremendous difference (and I hope this book will provide that kind of support to families experiencing ADHD today). I was lucky in that for many years my children spent every other weekend with their father, which gave me some time to myself. I treasured that time because it gave me the chance to connect with me the person rather than me the parent, me the carer and me the punch bag – and it was what helped me stay sane. I know many parents aren't afforded the luxury of 'me time', but if there's any way you can find even a couple of hours to yourself now and then, it's a great way to relax, de-stress and get yourself back on an even keel.

So, with that in mind, here are my five tips for self-preservation.

1. Don't blame yourself – or your child

ADHD is no one's fault. There's nothing you could have done to stop your child having ADHD, and there's nothing your child can do to help the fact that they have it. ADHD is a biological condition – it's not bad parenting, the food you feed them or anything else you have control over. Don't beat yourself up about it, be kind to yourself and your child, and don't let anyone tell you you're to blame – it's just one of those things.

2. Find out as much as you can about ADHD

It may be a cliché but knowledge really is power. The internet puts everything you could ever want to know at your fingertips, so do your research and find out as much as you can about ADHD and how it will affect your child. Dealing with medical professionals and schools is much easier when you understand what they're talking about and can hold your own in a discussion!

3. Join a support group

Feeling that you're all alone and no one else knows what you're going through is horrible – but it doesn't have to be that way. Almost every county has an ADHD support group where you can go along and meet other parents in a relaxed environment, and online groups and forums give you the opportunity to chat with other people whenever you want. I used to be very active on the Adders.org forum, which has discussion rooms for parents of ADHD children as well as adults with the disorder. It was refreshing to be able to talk about the problems I was experiencing with people who understood exactly what I was going through. There are also national organisations such as ADDISS that promote ADHD awareness and provide information, training and support. I've even started my own online ADHD parenting programme – the ADHD Kids Parents Club! You'll find a list of useful groups and organisations in Appendix 3: Resources at the end of this book.

4. Find time for yourself

I've already admitted that, as a single parent, I was very lucky because the children went to their father's every fortnight, giving me valuable time on my own. I appreciate it's not so easy for everyone, but if you can, call on the support of friends and family to give you a bit of a break. Even a couple of hours once a month can make a huge difference. Treat yourself to coffee with a friend, have a long soak in the bath, go swimming, join an exercise class, visit the shops or just curl up on the sofa with a book – whatever it takes to recharge your batteries. Don't be afraid to ask for help. Often we hold back for fear of what people might think, but you'll probably find there are people who are more than happy to look after your child for a while.

Depending on where you live, you may find that your local authority provides some sort of respite service, either for single sessions or short breaks. Find out what's available in your area via the IASS website: www. iassnetwork.org.uk.

5. Don't forget to have fun!

There was a time when almost every family outing seemed to be ruined by Daniel throwing a tantrum at the end of the day, and often it's easy to forget the fun you had beforehand and even easier to avoid going out again in case the same thing happens. Don't let your child's ADHD hold you back as a family. Enjoy being with the people you love, grit your teeth if people look disapprovingly at your child and make sure you hold on to the good memories. Take lots of photos of you and your child having fun – they're great to look back at when you're having a bad day!

For the last 18 years my role has been to do whatever it takes to get Daniel to a place where he can manage his life successfully. The struggle hasn't been easy, and it has taken its toll on me. Following Daniel's first exclusion I suffered depression and needed a course of anti-depressants to get me back on track. At the time I was studying for a degree, and the stress of juggling coursework and lectures with looking after a hyperactive child was intense. Fortunately, a good friend helped out by looking after Daniel while I attended college. It wasn't easy for her, though, as she often came into the firing line for Daniel's aggression – on one occasion I had to leave a lecture early as she'd had to barricade herself in the bathroom because an angry Daniel was outside the door, armed with a plastic guitar, threatening to kill her simply because she hadn't let him have his own way! (I actually ended up doing my dissertation – a half-hour radio documentary – on ADHD, and you can find a link to it in Appendix 3.)

At the time of Daniel's second exclusion I was running my own business, having given up a well-paid job to better support Daniel's needs. He was struggling in school at the time, and I realised I needed more flexibility than paid employment offered; I was forever having to leave work early to collect him from school after a bad lunchtime. However, trying to run a business and care for an angry, depressed ten-year-old boy was really difficult, and both the business and my health suffered. This time, as well as descending into the pits of depression, the stress caused a flare-up of previously undiagnosed arthritis in my knee (partly caused by surgery many years earlier), which made life difficult for a few months.

I guess in many ways I've had it easy, though. My circumstances – studying, self-employment – meant that I was able to carry on, with the support of friends and family, following the exclusions. Had I been in employment, I would have had to leave my job with immediate effect, which could have had devastating consequences on my state of mind and future prospects and our family finances. I really feel for parents who have to take that course of action. It's already tough enough bringing up a child with special needs; when the withdrawal of education leads to major life changes, it could be enough to tip you over the edge.

It's also had an effect on my relationships. When you have a child with ADHD, you are constantly living on edge because you know it could take just the tiniest thing for them to explode and you never quite know what might happen. Friends with their own children have had to accept that Daniel could be unpredictable in their company, and I've been fortunate to have a couple of friends who have seen past the ADHD and stuck with us through thick and thin.

Partners haven't had it so easy, however. I separated from Katie and Daniel's father when the children were young, for many reasons – some of which may be explained by his own subsequent diagnosis with ADHD. Although I had a couple of boyfriends after that, it was always difficult introducing them to Daniel because of his fear of change, and when I did finally meet someone and settle down, moving counties to get married, it was a complete disaster. My new husband had a child of his own and, as everyone moving into a step-family knows, blending a new family unit is never easy; when one of the children involved has a disability like ADHD, it's nigh on impossible. My daughter and I have come to understand Daniel and to learn techniques to cope when he's having a bad day, but it's asking a lot to expect two people without the experience – and the blood bond – to deal with such behaviour. There were many situations where meltdowns happened simply because the new members of our family hadn't yet learned to walk away from Daniel when he was showing signs of stress, and family days out usually ended in tears. I left the marriage after only two years, and although that wasn't entirely because of Daniel and his ADHD, it certainly played a big part.

Fortunately, I met a lovely man who has accepted Daniel just as he is, who respects him and has patience and time for him, and Daniel has responded well and respects him in return. We've had the odd moment, but finally we are a family unit that's as close to normal, whatever that is, as I think we'll ever get – and that makes us all happy.

However, the overwhelming emotion I've felt throughout my experience has been sadness for Daniel – for the upheaval he's experienced, the absence of friendships, the lack of invitations, the missed opportunities. It's difficult watching every other child in the class going to birthday parties when your own child is not welcome; it's heart-breaking when your own child tells you he's so miserable he'd rather be dead. All you can do is make family life as fun as possible, include as many experiences as the budget allows and do your best to compensate for the lack of a social life with his peers. We're not well-off by any means, but over the years we've enjoyed things as diverse as scuba diving, trips to the zoo, quad bikes, museum trips and rifle shooting, all to give Daniel a bit of fun in a controlled environment and the chance to improve his self-esteem.

So parenting Daniel has been challenging – heart-breaking at times – but it's also had its upside. My motivation for originally writing this book was simply to write a book – I felt I had something to contribute to the world, and I hoped maybe our experience would help other parents. At the time a friend and fellow author said to me, 'Once your book is out there your life will change in ways you can't begin to imagine,' and I laughed at her! After all, it was just one little book, about our story. How was it going to change anything? But within a couple of weeks of the book coming out I had an email from a parent thanking me for giving her hope that there was 'light at the end of the tunnel', which was the best feedback I could ever receive.

Publication of the book also resulted in some media coverage for Daniel and me. We were interviewed on local radio, I've spoken out against ADHD doubters on BBC Five Live and LBC, and we've been featured in our local newspaper, *SEN Magazine* and *Take a Break*. We even got a double-page spread in *Bella* magazine! Best of all, Olympic gymnast and *Strictly Come Dancing* winner Louis Smith came to our house for breakfast one day, part of filming for a TV programme for Channel 5 called *My Secret Past: Living with ADHD*. It was amazing to meet Louis, a lovely young man who freely admitted he still struggled to cope with the condition, and it gave Daniel a lot of inspiration.

I was also invited to speak about my experience at a conference in Liverpool. Little me standing up in front of 120 medical and educational professionals – who'd have thought it! But I really enjoyed the day and since then I have spoken at many events around the country, sharing our story and passing on the strategies that I've found useful.

This led me to want to do more to help other families struggling with ADHD, and in 2014 I trained as a coach and started working directly with parents, coaching and mentoring them under the name ADHD Kids. As far as I am concerned, ADHD isn't caused by bad parenting, but it can cause parents to lose confidence in their abilities, and as a result parenting can suffer. By helping parents build their confidence, I give them more opportunity to support their kids to reach their potential. I ran an ADHD Inspiration Day in 2014, organise workshops for teachers and have also launched an online ADHD parenting programme which is providing support to hundreds of parents around the country. At times it felt like ADHD was beating me to the ground, but now I'm using the ADHD stick to help other families.

So that's what it's been like for me as a parent. I was interested to hear from Katie and Daniel about how ADHD has affected life from their perspective, and the conversations we had were very revealing. I'm going to hand over to them now – the next few pages are their words, their stories and their insights into life with a child with ADHD.

ADHD from a Sibling's Perspective

Katie's Story

It's not always been easy having a brother with ADHD, but I don't feel it's meant I've missed out on anything; after all, it's all I've ever known, so the way we have behaved as a family because of it is just normal for me. I suppose it would have been nice growing up not having to worry about upsetting Daniel – because at times he's been very easy to wind up, and that's caused him to flip – but regardless of how he is and how we've had to behave around him, he is still my brother and I love him. I do remember lots of family days when we had a good time and it was – well…not ruined by Daniel, but there was something that caused him to blow up and you end up remembering that, the bad bit, rather than all the good things that happened.

I've often felt I've had to hold back on what I wanted to say in case it upset Daniel and made him flip. I've often got scared seeing the way he could explode at adults and it worried me that he might do the same to me, so I'd hold back rather than cause a meltdown. As I've got older, though – and a bit more mouthy! – I've started to speak my mind more and he has flipped at me a few times. Sometimes I've just got so sick of having to keep quiet that I've provoked him and that has caused some big fights. Not that it happens often, because once Daniel's flipped at you a couple of times you tend to try to stop it happening again!

I remember my birthday parties were always quite stressful for me, which is sad. I wanted Daniel involved but I was always worried what might happen if my friends managed to upset him. He quite often acted really silly, played up a lot and my friends were fine about it – in fact, they didn't understand why it made me so upset, they were happy to ignore him and it wasn't a big deal – but it used to really upset me.

My friends did notice that I behaved differently towards Daniel than they did with their siblings. There'd be times when he wanted to join in with me and my friends and I didn't want him to, but it was easier to let him than to say no and risk a meltdown. And even when I did want him involved, I was always on edge in case he flipped off with my friends.

One of my best friends has a brother with ADHD and we are probably closer because of it. It's good having someone to talk to outside the family who understands how I feel, and often we can understand each other without having to find the words to express our feelings. I also talked to my friend's mum a lot, because of course she understood things more than my other friends' parents did. I didn't really talk to teachers about Daniel because I felt they had no experience of it and wouldn't understand, but my grandma has always been very supportive and we are really close.

We've all been hurt physically by Daniel when he's had a meltdown. Fortunately, he's much calmer now, he rarely explodes, but we'll never fully understand how it feels to be him in a meltdown. We do understand that it's nothing personal – he doesn't mean to hurt anyone, it's just that his anger takes over and anyone who gets in the way can get hurt. He just can't stop what happens when he flips, even with people he cares about.

One time in particular I remember we were on holiday and Mum and Grandma had gone out for a couple of hours. We'd made friends with some other kids on holiday and Daniel wanted to prove he was old enough to be left with me – I was nearly 15 and he was 11. We were playing in a ball pool and one of the other kids started annoying Daniel, and I could tell he was getting really wound-up and angry. We'd only known this boy a few days, and I was really worried that if Daniel flipped and hurt him, it could end up in big trouble – the boy's parents might call the police or anything – and I didn't want Daniel to get into trouble because I knew he couldn't help how he was behaving. So I put myself between Daniel and this boy, literally pulled Daniel away so he could try to calm down and he kicked my legs to bits in the process and it hurt – it really hurt. But at the time I wasn't worried about getting hurt – it was more important to protect him and get him away so he could calm down, so he wouldn't get into worse trouble. Afterwards he was really upset, he went to bed and cried for hours because he was angry with himself for hurting me.

Actually, that's the worst thing about when he gets angry – how upset he is afterwards, when he's calmed down and realised what happened. He's so upset he literally can't look at you or speak to you, and seeing him that upset hurts me more than any physical pain.

We have to forgive him when he does awful things and hurts people; our lives would be horrible if we couldn't. He never does things maliciously – he's always said that he literally can't help his behaviour, it's like he's watching someone else and there's nothing he can do to stop it. So we have always forgiven him, but I think he finds it much harder to forgive himself. In fact, I don't think he'd ever consider behaving aggressively if he didn't have ADHD – he's pretty laid-back really, not the kind of person who would lash out. I don't think he would react in that way to anything if he had a choice.

I suppose Daniel must have needed more attention than I got, especially when we were younger, but I never felt jealous of that. I understood that sometimes he needed more attention, but Mum did a great job of sharing her time between us and she was always there to help me with homework, give me a hug or watch telly with me, even when Daniel was having a really bad time. We've always been a very close family, we've always done lots together and I've never felt 'back seated' because of Daniel's ADHD.

I know sometimes I behave a bit selfishly by deliberately saying things I know will annoy him, but generally I think I've grown up being more considerate than most kids about how my actions could affect other people. I'd like to think I'm a very open-minded person anyway, but I think I am more understanding of people who have behavioural difficulties or other mental health issues because I've grown up with a brother with a disability. I think I'm more able to adapt to difficult situations because I've been doing that since I was small. If I'm with a group of people facing some tricky situation, I tend to panic less than the others – even if I'm scared – because I've been in some quite extreme situations with Daniel and coping with them then has made me more capable now. I can normally see a way of dealing with things, however difficult they are.

I've recently graduated with a degree in psychology, in which I specialised in my third year in child psychology. My choice of psychology for A Level, and further study, has been influenced by my family life and wanting to know more about what makes us human, and, more specifically, the reasons that some people are different. I am particularly interested in this with regard to children, as it both explains my experience of living with Daniel and gives me in-depth knowledge so I can help others. I have just begun a further two years at university, during which time I will be studying education, and will become a qualified early years practitioner and a qualified primary school teacher. I hope to be able to use my experience of growing up with Daniel, and the theoretical knowledge of my degree, to help me to deal with, and hopefully help, any children I come across with special needs. I am still exploring my options and have a long way to go before being a proper teacher, but at present I am definitely in the mindset of exploring the possibilities of teaching in a special needs school, or progressing through teaching to the position of SENCO, in order to help as many families as possible who have a child with special needs.

I guess one of the nice things about Daniel is that he's never taken himself too seriously and he has quite a – how shall I put this? – bizarre streak to his personality which makes him a very entertaining person to have around. He has a unique perspective on life and during the good times that has made family life fun. It could be that he would have been that way anyway – he might just be someone with a very amusing take on life – but he's certainly never been a boring brother. In fact, he's probably more boring now as a teenager than he's ever been!

Because we've always been a close family Mum has been very open with me about Daniel and his disability, so I understood the problems from an early age and that's actually meant Daniel and I have been really close as brother and sister. Actually, because of everything we've been through together, we're close as friends too – perhaps closer than my friends are with their siblings. I think it's really important for parents to be open with siblings about ADHD. I'm still really protective towards Daniel too. OK, I'm probably too small to step in and protect him physically these days, but I would still do whatever I could to stop him getting into trouble, even if it meant I got hurt in the process. Within the family we know to step back and let him calm down if he's getting stressed, and if he does flip, we know we'll all be OK once he's calmed down, but if that happened outside the home, the consequences could be much harsher and I wouldn't want anything bad to happen to him.

I'm really pleased my mum has found her new partner because he gets on really well with Daniel, and Daniel actually respects him and listens to him too. We were a single-parent family for a long time so it's nice to have that proper family thing going on now.

Regardless of how Daniel and his ADHD may have affected my life, it's just what I'm used to and I wouldn't want it any other way. Yes, there have been bad times but there have been plenty of good times too and it certainly hasn't put a negative spin on my childhood. If someone close to you has a behavioural problem like ADHD, don't try to fight against it – accept it, that's just the way it is. I've never wanted things to be any different because Daniel is my brother and I love him.

ADHD from the Child's Perspective

Daniel's Story

When I was younger, I think maybe I used my ADHD as an excuse. I couldn't help how I behaved but saying it was because I had ADHD was easier than trying to stop the bad behaviour. I remember I was really bad sometimes – throwing chairs at the teacher, for example – but for me that was just normal behaviour, I didn't know any different. It didn't feel like a problem for me when I was young and I seemed to be quite popular with the other children too.

I don't remember the first time I was excluded. I was at school and then it was the holidays and then I was at another school [the Pupil Referral Unit], only this time it was just me and a woman and another woman and sometimes another kid. It was like being at school but without all the fun stuff – I didn't like the lack of social interaction with other kids my age. We didn't do much work there either and I think I fell quite a long way behind, which caused some problems later.

Then we moved and I went to a proper school again and it went fairly well for a while – there were blips, and they weren't particularly small blips either, but I did OK and I had a good group of friends too. But being in a big class again was noisy and distracting, and it was difficult to get help from the teachers. There were two other boys in my class who had behavioural difficulties like me and only one teacher and a teaching assistant, and it meant there wasn't really enough help for us all.

Because I'd missed a lot of schooling while I was at the unit, I had problems with writing and spelling, and that was really frustrating because I wanted to be working with my friends – the bright kids – and I was stuck with the slower ones. I wanted to do well at school but I was always struggling. The noise and the distraction and my own lack of confidence meant that I felt I would fail if I tried to do the work and that would make me angry, so I tried to avoid doing it – but the teacher made me, and that just made me angry anyway!

When I was excluded for the second time, I was annoyed with myself – I'd let myself down by messing up so badly. I wasn't in control, I'd blown up and I lost not only school but also the group of friends I'd made. I know I could have tried to stay in touch but it was just very awkward.

The time with the home tutors was the worst; it was terrible. I was stuck at home with no exposure to anything and the only people I saw during the day were my mum and a tutor. I really missed being with other kids. It was incredibly boring and frustrating, I didn't seem to be learning anything and I just wanted to kill my mum because we were stuck together and driving each other mad! *(Note from Mum: the feeling was mutual!)*

Going back to school – the special school – was good because I was with people my own age again. I got on well with the kids at the junior school, although I found it harder at senior school and I got on better with the teachers than the other boys. The environment was great, though – classes were smaller than mainstream – not too much, not too little – and the teachers understood what ticked me off and what to do if I was having a bad day.

There've been times when I thought I'd never achieve anything in life, but I did come out of school with a few GCSEs and a whole lot of skills and experiences. After school I went to a college where I did IT and I passed with merit – now there's something I never thought I'd say.

I used to have a lot of meltdowns and it was like tunnel vision – once you're annoyed with someone or something you want to hurt them and that becomes your only goal. It's like being a train on tracks. When most people get angry, they can choose whether they explode – go into the dark tunnel – or flick the points, change direction and find another way to go. For me the tracks went straight into the tunnel – there were no diversions. It's dark, it's black and bad things happen there, but you as a person don't know what you're doing – it's the anger inside that controls you and there's no stopping what it does till you come out the other side of the tunnel and calm down. It's like you're a passenger on the train – you know you don't want to go into the tunnel, but there's nothing you can do to stop the train; you just have to sit and watch everything happen.

After a meltdown I always felt really upset because I didn't want anything bad to happen, but there was nothing I could do to stop it. It was really scary seeing myself lose it and I hated the way I felt afterwards – I was always so sorry for everything I'd done – but there was nothing I could do to stop it happening again, it wasn't in my control.

Medication helped by extending the tracks before the tunnel entrance. It gave me more time to put on the brakes or find a diversion, and sometimes I could stop the train going into the tunnel – but sometimes it still sucked me in.

As I've got older, I've learned to control the anger much better and I haven't had a proper meltdown for years. Don't get me wrong, I still get angry – but I know when it's happening and can normally calm myself down. Usually, that means walking away from whoever is annoying me, or telling them to leave me alone. And when I do blow, I'm able to contain it a lot better, by swearing or hitting a desk or wall rather than a person.

Medication really helped me feel like I was more in control – it mellowed me out a bit, made me less jumpy and gave me a longer fuse. I used to need it because I would get wound-up too easily otherwise – I wouldn't last the day without it. But I think it was also a bit of a depressant – it made me more serious and less likely to want to mess around. It made me boring! There were days when I didn't take it and those days I felt much happier, but I knew I needed it at school to help me keep calm and not get so stressed out with the other kids. I got on really well with some of the teachers at my school, but it made me sad that they only knew me as 'Daniel on drugs' – but I thought they probably wouldn't like the person I was without medication.

I've not been on medication for over a year now – I took it when I had my GCSE exams but then stopped during the holidays and haven't had any since. Recently, I went back to my school to visit the teachers and I was so pleased to find that after all my worry about them not liking the real me they actually did like me! That was really nice.

Something else that happened was that the doctor said I have Asperger's as well as ADHD. She asked me how I felt about that, but I just said it didn't make a difference what labels you put on me, I'm still me. I know my Asperger's makes me socially awkward but I actually see that as just part of my personality, it's just the way I am. I don't feel I have to work harder at doing things because it's just the way it has always been.

I don't regret being on medication for all those years. It definitely helped me to stay in school and to learn how to manage my ADHD. Without the medication, I find it harder to concentrate, but the benefit is that I am me, I'm not a zombie any more. I eat a lot more too!

Having ADHD is not great. There are lots of positives in my life now, but I know that if I didn't have ADHD, life would have been a lot better. Having a label isn't good – I know I'm a nice person but people hear that I've got ADHD and instantly think that I must be trouble –

and that reputation seems to follow me everywhere, even though I'm quite a nice person really! I know I've done some bad things but I'm older and calmer now – but people just think of me as that bad kid with ADHD. There are no benefits from having ADHD and I think anyone who says there are is lying.

I'm much more in control now. I'm able to hold back and not blow up so much. I used to think I'd always need medication to help me control myself in certain situations and I'm pleased that I've been able to stop taking it and be OK.

I'm 18 now but I feel like I'm a few years older – going through so much and having to deal with it all has made me grow up quickly. When I was younger, I missed out on being part of a group of friends and I feel like I missed out on being a kid in some ways too. However, going to college helped me feel a lot more confident and I made some good friends, and I have a big group of friends through gaming too. I don't really know what I want to do for a career – I'm looking for an apprenticeship or job right now, probably in business administration or IT. Right now I'm just enjoying being a normal teenager, doing stuff with friends.

I'd like people to realise that kids with ADHD can be nice and they shouldn't be defined by their disability. I think ADHD probably suppresses my personality somewhat and I would be even nicer if I didn't have it. But you just have to be the person you're meant to be – don't let ADHD hold you back, just get on with it and deal with it. That goes for parents too – it's not always nice having a kid with ADHD, but you just have to deal with it, like my mum has.

Where We Are Now –
and Where We're Going

Saturday 9th August 2014: So Dan is having a weekend in London to go to a computer gaming event. On his own. So far he's managed to get from Didcot to London, navigate the Underground (with some help!) and find his accommodation. Very proud of him!

So now we come to the present day. I've always worried about what Daniel would do with his life. As a child, he changed career ambitions every week – zoo keeper, chef, computer games designer, teaching assistant. He's now 18 and looking for an apprenticeship or job, something to do with business administration or IT.

He spent the last year of his education at a local college, and as well as passing a BTEC IT course with merit, it was a massively important year for him in terms of personal development. Going from a tiny school of

60 boys to a huge college with thousands of students was a big deal, and I wasn't sure how well Daniel would cope. The college was really helpful and ensured that tutors knew his limitations and support was in place from day one. They even set up a 'Time Out' system so he could leave the classroom if he was feeling antsy, and he appreciated having some autonomy over managing his behaviour. However, the biggest shift came in social interactions. Having spent five years with other boys on the special needs spectrum, Daniel was suddenly thrust into the world of neurotypical people. After an initial lack of self-esteem, he has grown in confidence and is now a fine young man – polite, intelligent, entertaining and caring – although he still swears more than I'd like!

When Daniel decided to stop taking his medication, I was quite concerned about how he would cope – especially when he started at college. He'd been drug-free at home during weekends and school holidays for several months, but the idea of him out in the big wide world was another prospect entirely. What worried me most wasn't Daniel himself but other people – or, rather, his reaction to other people. I was scared that without medication, he'd be more easy to wind up, quicker to anger, and that could lead to trouble. Amazingly, though, he's coped really well without it. All those years on Ritalin gave him the opportunity to learn strategies and techniques to manage his emotions, and he's very good at backing away from a situation if he feels the anger brewing. His appetite has returned and although I hadn't realised the medication was dulling his personality, it's been lovely seeing this passionate, funny, loving young man emerge from the fog. OK, he still has his daft moments, he taps and fidgets like nothing on earth and trying to get him to sit down and fill in a job application is a nightmare, but generally he copes so well now without medication.

He's much more organised these days, and relatively tidy too. His bag and shoes are always put back in the same place and he never loses his keys – something I could certainly learn from! He's still quite forgetful – give him a list of three things to do and he might manage two, if you're lucky – but he's developed routines for himself that keep him on track. For the boy who used to forget what he was doing halfway through cleaning his teeth, that's quite an achievement!

Over the last few years I've tried hard to foster a sense of independence in Daniel. Through necessity, he hadn't had much – when you can't be sure your child will leave the house and return without having exploded and thumped someone, you tend not to let them out too often! But he's much more mature now, and seems far more in control of his actions. He's started doing a bit of cooking at home – so far he's only mastered scrambled eggs, pasta and Pot Noodles, but it's a start. He also has his own bank account and is responsible for what he spends his money on (although he does make a lot of impulsive purchases!). We've had some problems with smoking and weed – but I've tried to manage it sympathetically and it's not become an issue. I know Daniel is still grieving for his father and this is his way of coping, so as long as it doesn't become uncontrollable I'm happy to take a hands-off attitude and let him find his own way.

One of my biggest concerns about Daniel has always been his lack of friends and a social life. As a toddler, he did have a small group of friends, but the way the birthdays fell meant they all started school a year before he did, and although he had a few friends in infant school, he was never invited to tea or to parties. I think the parents were wary of having him around without me there to step in if he flipped – and who could blame them? When we moved, he had a group of friends and one best friend, but after his second exclusion the relationship became strained and they haven't seen each other for years. Daniel struggled to find friends at special school and he freely admitted that he found kids his own age a bit dull; he was far closer to the twenty-something teaching assistants.

I felt sad that he didn't have friends or a 'normal' teenage social life and I tried to find activities for him to do, but his own reluctance to try new things often put a barrier in the way. He tried youth club and the local kids' swimming session but had problems with some boys who deliberately wound him up to the point of meltdown (and then cried foul when he exploded). For a while he was scared to go out in our home town because he thought everyone knew about him and would make his life difficult. Gradually, I began to encourage him to go out more on his own and he started with a bus trip to the cinema. OK, he got off the bus a stop early coming home, but other than that it was a successful trip! We also took him to London Victoria and put him on a train to Brighton to visit his sister, who was at university there. She met him at the other end and he spent a few days down there, doing teenage things without any 'adult' supervision. (Katie, 18 at the time, was an adult, of course, but you know what I mean!) He had a great few days away and got on really well with her friends.

Outside of college, most of Daniel's time was spent sitting in his bedroom playing on the computer or watching gaming championships online. And, in fact, it is this that has been the real turning point for him.

One morning last year he appeared in the lounge with an announcement. 'Mum, I'm going to London. On my own.' Shock horror – I didn't know what to think! Turns out one of his YouTube heroes, Jesse Cox, was organising a gaming get-together at County Hall and Daniel was determined he was going to attend – despite never having travelled so far on his own. We bought train tickets and arranged accommodation, and on the day I drove him to Didcot Parkway and put him on the right train. I was really worried about how he was going to cope in London, all alone, but apart from a panicky phone call when one of the Underground lines was closed, and another to help me guide him to his accommodation (thank goodness for Google Maps!), he had a fantastic weekend and came home having made a friend too.

Then followed a trip to Coventry for the Insomnia gaming festival, where he met more of his gaming heroes and many of the people he'd been playing games with online. Another successful expedition, and this time he came home with a girlfriend! Since then he's travelled further afield and he regularly meets up with his gaming friends, a lovely bunch of people who have accepted Daniel, social awkwardness and all. Finally he feels accepted in the world and he has friends and a social life – and he's blossomed.

And then came the moment when my boy became a man. Galvanised by the coverage of the refugee crisis, in September 2015 I joined a local solidarity group with whom I travelled to the camp at Calais with supplies. I invited Daniel to join me and was surprised when he accepted. Over the following days I expected him to bail out – especially when I told him we had to be up at 4am – but he was adamant he was coming. He started the morning as a nerdy, anxious teenager, but by the end of the day he'd grown in so many ways. He struck up conversations with refugees from around the world, showing them empathy and compassion; he found practical solutions to problems; he encouraged other volunteers when they were running out of energy; and he demonstrated real leadership qualities. He's since returned many times and has made a real difference to the lives of hundreds of people. I couldn't be a more proud mum.

When he was younger, Daniel truly did seem like 'the boy from hell', and in many ways I feel we as a family have been to hell and back because of his ADHD. Ten years ago – even five years ago – I wouldn't have predicted that things would be going as well as they are now. At times family life was a daily ordeal and all I could see for Daniel was a future of anger and violence. I couldn't imagine he would ever succeed at school, or get a job, or find a girlfriend, or settle down. But now, while we're still at the very beginning of his journey into adulthood, I can see a far brighter future ahead and I wish Daniel – and all the other children like him – all the success they deserve.

A Note from the Author

I really hope you found our story interesting – and that you've picked up some useful information too. As an author, I rely on word-of-mouth recommendations and reviews to help me get my story out there and (I hope) help other families struggling with an ADHD child. If you have enjoyed this book (or even if you haven't!), please do consider leaving a review on either Amazon or GoodReads. It doesn't have to be very long and I will be forever grateful!

The following pages include lots of useful information for families dealing with ADHD, including:

- the diagnostic criteria used to diagnose ADHD

- tips on how to claim Disability Living Allowance for your child (still available for anyone aged 0–16 at the time of writing)

- recommended websites and books, plus a list of support groups

- a glossary of terms used in this book.

Appendix 1

The Diagnostic Criteria of ADHD

As explained in the book, there are two sets of diagnostic criteria used to diagnose ADHD: DSM-5 and ICD-10. DSM-5 is the one used most often in the UK.

DSM-5 Criteria for ADHD

Although DSM-5 is a tool devised by the American Psychiatric Association, it is the tool most commonly used in the UK to diagnose ADHD. It lists a number of symptoms, and to be diagnosed with either ADHD Inattentive or ADHD Hyperactive/Compulsive, children need to have displayed at least six symptoms regularly, for at least six months and in two different settings (e.g. home and school). Children with ADHD Combined need to display at least six symptoms from each list. The following lists will give you an idea of what the symptoms are.

Inattentiveness

- Short attention span
- Easily distracted
- Often make silly mistakes, e.g. in schoolwork
- Forgetful and disorganised
- Not able to focus on boring tasks
- Not able to listen to instructions, or carry them out
- Flitting from one activity to another

Hyperactivity/impulsiveness

- Unable to sit still
- Constant fidgeting
- Calling things out
- Difficulty concentrating on tasks
- Excessive chatting
- Not able to wait their turn
- Doing without thinking
- Interrupting

You can view the full diagnostic criteria, as well as a symptom checklist, at www.cdc.gov/ncbddd/adhd/ diagnosis.html.

ICD-10 Diagnostic Criteria for Hyperkinetic Disorder

The World Health Organization has its own 'version' of ADHD, called Hyperkinetic Disorder, and this is diagnosed using a tool called ICD-10. The symptoms of Hyperkinetic Disorder are similar to those of ADHD Combined and children need to show both inattentive and hyperactive/impulsive symptoms to get a diagnosis. However, Hyperkinetic Disorder is only really diagnosed for very severe cases, and most children with ADHD-like behaviours in the UK will have been diagnosed under the DSM criteria. However, if you are interested in learning more about Hyperkinetic Disorder you can find the full diagnostic criteria at www.who.int/classifications/icd/en/GRNBOOK.pdf.

Appendix 2

Disability Living Allowance

Since 2013, the government has been gradually phasing out Disability Living Allowance (DLA) and replacing it with a new benefit, Personal Independence Payments (PIP).

However, at the time of writing DLA is still available for children aged 0–16. For more information and to start a claim, download a claim form from www.gov.uk/disability-living-allowance-children or call 0345 712 3456 to request a printed form.

It takes around 40 days for your application to be processed, and your child may need a medical assessment. If your application is successful, your allowance will be backdated to either the date your form was received or the date you requested the form on the phone…so it's definitely worth phoning to request one rather than downloading it!

Young people over the age of 16 will need to apply for PIP at www.gov.uk/pip.

If your child is currently receiving DLA, they will be transferred to PIP when they reach 16. However, transitions are being phased in gradually, with different postcodes being transferred at different times. To find out when your child will be transferred to the new benefit, visit www.gov.uk/pip-checker.

Claiming Disability Living Allowance (DLA) for your child is an emotional, difficult process. Although the application form is very long, it is quite clear and straightforward to complete; however, you do have to picture your child in the most negative light. Here are a few tips for filling in the form, and also a guide to some of the questions. There's no guarantee that you will get the allowance – it's becoming increasingly hard for anyone with a disability to get financial help, and with 'hidden' disabilities like ADHD it's even more difficult – but having applied successfully for Daniel, I hope this information will help you.

Take your time

The form is very long and daunting, and if you try to complete it in one go, you may find it overwhelming. Try to fill in a few bits every day over a week.

Think negatively

This goes against everything you try to do, I know, but you really do need to think about how your child is on their very worst day. Don't include anything positive on the form because that could jeopardise your application.

Talk to family and friends

As parents, we just do what we have to do every day, so it can be hard to see what additional care and support we actually give our children. Talk to family and friends because they often have a more objective view of things and can point out some areas of your child's behaviour and care that you'd never considered.

Keep a diary

You might find it useful to keep a diary for a week before you fill in the DLA form. Write down everything you do for your child, including washing and dressing, mealtimes, medication, night-time routines and behaviour. This will give you a clearer picture of just how much you help your child – you might be surprised!

Write it like a story

The best way to demonstrate what life is like for you and your child is to tell it how it is. Don't worry about writing in a formal way – just write the story of your child's day.

Take a copy of the form

If you are successful with your DLA claim, you'll have to do it all over again in three years' time, even if your child's condition hasn't changed. Take a copy of the completed form so you can use it as reference material for future applications. It's also worth having a copy just in case your application gets lost in the post.

Completing the form

The first 20 questions on the DLA application form are fairly straightforward – they collect your contact information and your child's educational and medical details. (Question 19 is a signed statement where you summarise the care you give your child – you might want to come back to this question once you've completed the rest of the form.)

The next 35 questions are about the care your child needs. Because the same form is used for all children with a disability, a lot of the questions will not apply, but the following information might be helpful.

Q21: List the child's disabilities

Include your child's full diagnosis (including any co-morbidities), any medication your child takes, how often they take it and any additional therapies they're receiving – for example, cognitive therapy, anger management.

Q32–36: Guidance or supervision outdoors

Many ADHD children need constant supervision outdoors because they are likely to run across roads without looking, get distracted and wander off, are liable to run away, aren't aware of 'stranger danger', can become violent or aggressive towards people or property, can't follow simple instructions, can get lost easily.

Q37: Help needed to get in, out or settled in bed during the day

Do you have big problems getting your child up in the mornings? Do you have to constantly wake them or encourage them to get up – more than with other children? Include that here.

Q38: Help and encouragement to use the toilet during the day

ADHD children often get so distracted they forget to go to the toilet. If your child needs reminding to go to the loo or wash their hands or frequently wets themselves because they forget to go, mention it here.

Q40: Help or encouragement with washing

Does your child get in the shower or bath but forget to actually wash themselves? Do you need to remind them to brush their teeth, wash their hands, etc.? Do they have to have a rigid bath-time routine, or refuse to wash altogether? If so, mention it here.

Q41: Help with dressing

Things to consider here include getting distracted during dressing, inability to dress themselves at all, sensitivity to certain fabrics, poor fine-motor skills when doing up buttons and zips, obsessions with certain items of clothing/colours of clothing.

Q42: Encouragement, prompting or help with eating and drinking

Again, distraction is often a factor here – do you need to remind your child to finish their meal? Children with autistic traits may often have specific food obsessions, and you can also include any special diets your child is on because of their condition – for example, wheat-free, dairy-free, additive-free.

Q43: Help taking medication

Most ADHD medications are controlled substances, so it's essential you supervise your child taking them. From my own experience, Daniel used to struggle to swallow his medication and needed encouragement – otherwise he would spit it out. You will also need to remind your child when medication is due, especially with a lunchtime dose.

Q46: Difficulty with speaking

Some ADHD children find it difficult to express themselves and get frustrated, or speak very quickly and are difficult to understand. If this applies to your child, include it here.

Q47: Difficulty with communication

Does your child need you to repeat instructions several times? Do they have a literal understanding of language and struggle to decipher phrases and sayings? Do you sometimes need to draw pictures to help them understand? Do they have problems understanding facial expressions and gestures? Does your child often blurt out rude words, or does their aggressive behaviour cause communication problems because other people don't know how to talk to them? Anything along those lines can be included here.

Q49: Supervision during the day

All children with ADHD need extra supervision during the day because their behaviour can put them or other people in danger. In this section you need to explain everything about your child's behaviour, including tantrums and meltdowns, aggression and violence, destruction of objects, hurting themselves and other people, frustration, impulsive behaviour, verbal abuse, distraction, lack of concentration, risk-taking behaviour, fearlessness, bullying (or being the victim of bullying).

Q50: Help with their development

This question is about how your child's ADHD affects their normal development. You can include lots of information from previous questions about personal hygiene, mealtimes, outdoor supervision, etc., but also focus on things like their inability to play with other children, problems following instructions, inappropriate behaviour, lack of understanding of the world around them, friendships, social skills (do they get on with children their own age/younger/older/adults?), school progress.

Q51: Help at school

Include any additional help they need at school, including lunchtime medication, help getting changed for PE, reminding about the toilet, concentration issues. Speak to teachers if you're not sure what help your child needs at school.

Q52: Help or encouragement with hobbies

Think about both the hobbies and activities your child does and the hobbies they'd like to do if help was available. For example, they may like swimming but you can't take them because they need more supervision than you can provide, they may not be able to go to youth club without someone to supervise, art is difficult because of concentration issues, they need help getting changed for football. It could be there are things your child would like to do but they lack the confidence because of their ADHD and would need more encouragement than other children.

Q53: Help at night

If your child goes to sleep very late, wakes in the night, sleepwalks, roams the house, wakes up other family members, has nightmares, wets the bed or gets up to play at midnight, include it all here.

The final section gives you the opportunity to include anything you haven't already mentioned. Remember, any help your child needs must be help that a neurotypical child of the same age would not need.

Appendix 3

Resources

Information and advice on special needs education, school exclusions, Statements and DLA

Ace Education
Information on exclusions, Statements and the educational rights of children with special needs.

www.ace-ed.org.uk/advice-about-education-for-parents

Tel: 0300 0115 142

Cerebra
Cerebra is a charity for children with neurological conditions. They have a very useful handbook on claiming Disability Living Allowance.

http://w3.cerebra.org.uk/help-and-information/guides-for-parents/dla-guide

Tel: 0800 328 1159

Contact a Family
For families with disabled children.

www.cafamily.org.uk

Tel: 0808 808 3555

The Council for Disabled Children (CDC)
The Council for Disabled Children is the umbrella body for the disabled children's sector in England. Very useful information on legal issues and government policies relating to children with disabilities.

www.councilfordisabledchildren.org.uk

Tel: 0207 843 1900

Government guidance on exclusions
http://bit.ly/1KnEgpR

Government guidance on children with special educational needs
www.gov.uk/children-with-special-educational-needs/overview

Information on tribunals for children with Special Educational Needs and Disabilities (SEND)

www.gov.uk/special-educational-needs-disability-tribunal

Information, Advice and Support Services Network (formerly Parent Partnership)

www.iassnetwork.org.uk

Tel: 0207 843 6051

IPSEA

Independent Parental Special Education Advice – national charity providing free legally based advice to families who have children with special educational needs.

www.ipsea.org.uk

General advice line: 0800 018 4016
Tribunal helpline: 0845 602 9579

SOS SEN

Independent helpline offering advice and help to parents negotiating the complicated maze of Special Educational Needs.

www.sossen.org.uk

Tel: 0208 538 3731 (helpline open Monday–Friday, 9.30am–12.30pm and 2pm–5pm, term time only)

Special Needs Jungle
Information on a range of special needs issues – especially good on the Statement process.

specialneedsjungle.com

ADHD organisations

ADDers
One of the longest-standing online ADHD groups in the UK, ADDers aims to promote awareness of ADHD and provide information and practical help to sufferers, both adults and children, and their families in the UK and around the world.

www.adders.org

ADDISS
The National Attention Deficit Disorder Information and Support Service, providing people-friendly information and resources about ADHD to anyone who needs assistance – parents, sufferers, teachers or health professionals.

www.addiss.co.uk

Tel: 0208 952 2800

ADHD Foundation
Charity based in Liverpool whose mission is to work in partnership with individuals, families, statutory and

voluntary agencies, to increase understanding, promote inclusion in mental health, education, employment and improve the life chances of those living with ADHD. Parenting courses and more.

www.adhdfoundation.org.uk

Tel: 0151 237 2661

ADHD Kids
My own website, providing information and support for parents of children with ADHD.

www.adhdkids.org.uk

ADHD Kids Online
ADHD parenting programme you can study in your own time.

www.adhdkidsonline.com

ADHD Pages from Hi2U
Articles on ADHD from Hi2u – an online community for people with hidden impairments.

www.adhd.org.uk

HACSG
The Hyperactive Children's Support Group – an organisation that advocates a medication-free approach to ADHD management through diet.

www.hacsg.org.uk

Tel: 01243 539966

National Autistic Society

As well as supporting and promoting the needs of autistic people, this charity has lots of information on other related conditions, including ADHD.

www.autism.org.uk

Tel: 0808 800 4104

Young Minds

Leading UK charity committed to improving the emotional well being and mental health of children and young people. Real life stories from children and young people with ADHD. Free telephone helpline for parents.

www.youngminds.org.uk

Tel: 0808 802 5544

The following website is actually run by a pharmaceutical company but is worth a look.

Living with ADHD

Lots of useful resources, including sections for parents and teens, downloadable mood diaries and workbooks. They also have a free phone app to help you keep a record of your child's behaviour and mood.

www.livingwithadhd.co.uk

Regional Support Groups

The ADDers.org website has a comprehensive list of local and regional support groups.

England: *www.adders.org/englandmap.htm*

Scotland: *www.adders.org/scotlandmap.htm*

Northern Ireland: *www.adders.org/nirelandmap.htm*

Wales: *www.adders.org/walesmap.htm*

Support groups in other countries are listed here: *www. adders.org/sgroups.html*

Recommended Books

The following are books that I have found useful.

Understanding ADHD: A Parent's Guide to Attention Deficit Hyperactivity Disorder in Children by Dr Christopher Green and Dr Kit Chee (Vermillion, 1997)

ADHD by Fintan O'Regan (Continuum International Publishing Group, 2007)

Only a Mother Could Love Him: How I Lived with and Triumphed over ADHD by Ben Polis (Hodder Paperbacks, 2005)

The Explosive Child: A New Approach for Understanding and Parenting Easily Frustrated, Chronically Inflexible Children by Ross W. Greene (Harper Paperbacks, 2010)

Marching to a Different Tune: Diary about an ADHD Boy by Jacky Fletcher (Jessica Kingsley Publishing, 1999)

Try and Make Me: A Revolutionary Program for Raising Your Defiant Child – without Losing Your Cool by Ray Levy, Bill O'Hanlon, Tyler Norris Goode (Rodale Press, 2004)

The Defiant Child: A Parent's Guide to Oppositional Defiant Disorder by Douglas Riley (Taylor Trade Publishing, 1997)

Multicoloured Mayhem: Parenting the Many Shades of Adolescents and Children with Autism, Asperger Syndrome and AD/HD by Jacqui Jackson (Jessica Kingsley Publishers, 2003)

A Volcano in My Tummy: Helping Children to Handle Anger by Eliane Whitehouse, Warwick Pudney (New Society Publishers, 1997)

———◆———

Finally…when I was studying for my degree I produced a half-hour radio documentary on ADHD. It features interviews with a top ADHD medical specialist, the founder of ADDers.org, an educational specialist, a special school and a celebrity ADHDer, and you can listen to it at http://adhdkids.org.uk/radio-documentary-adhd. Please do bear in mind that this was a university project so the quality is not of a professional standard!

Thanks to the following people for permission to post this documentary online:

BBC Radio 2

Fintan O'Regan

Simon Hensby/ADDers.org

More House School, Frensham, Surrey

Dr Billy Levin

A licence from PRS was obtained at the time of recording for the use of the music.

Appendix 4

Glossary

These are some of the terms and acronyms you're likely to encounter during your ADHD journey.

ADD: Attention Deficit Disorder (what ADHD is sometimes referred to as)

ADHD: Attention Deficit Hyperactivity Disorder

ASD: Autistic Spectrum Disorder

BESD: Behavioural, Emotional and Social Difficulties

BS: Behaviour Support

CAMHS: Child and Adolescent Mental Health Services

CD: Conduct Disorder, one of the co-morbidities that can accompany ADHD

DLA: Disability Living Allowance

EBD: Emotional and Behavioural Difficulties

Ed Psych/EP: Educational Psychologist

EHCP or EHC Plan: Education, Health and Care Plan

GP: General Practitioner

IEP: Individual Education Plan

LA: Local Authority

LEA: Local Education Authority (now part of the Local Authority)

LD: learning difficulties affecting development and ability to learn

Non-stimulants: certain types of ADHD medication including Strattera

NICE: the National Institute for Health and Clinical Excellence

OCD: Obsessive Compulsive Disorder

ODD: Oppositional Defiant Disorder

PCP: Pastoral Care Plan

PIP: Personal Independence Payment

PPS: Parent Partnership Service

Psycho-stimulants: stimulant medication for ADHD including Ritalin, Dexedrine and Adderall

SEN: special educational needs

SENCO: Special Educational Needs Co-ordinator

SEND: special educational needs and disabilities

SENDIST: Special Educational Needs Disability Tribunal

SEN Support: support for children with SEN in school, prior to being assessed for an EHC Plan

School Action: internal help provided by a school for a child with special needs (replaced by SEN Support)

School Action Plus: additional help for a child with special needs from external services such as Behaviour Support or the Ed Psych (replaced by SEN Support)

Statement of Special Educational Needs: a legally binding document that outlines a child's special needs and the support to be provided, which can also name a specific school (being replaced by Education, Health and Care Plans)

Statementing: the process that results in a Statement

Statutory Assessment: the assessment process leading to a Statement

References

1. Barkley, R. A. and Peters, H. (2012) 'The earliest known reference to ADHD in the medical literature? Melchior Adam Weikard's description in 1775 of "attention deficit" (Mangel der Aufmerksamkeit, Attentio Volubilis).' *Journal of Attention Disorders*, published online first, 8 February 2012.

2. Green, C. and Chee, K. (1997) *Understanding ADHD – A Parent's Guide to Attention Deficit Hyperactivity Disorder in Children*. Vermillion Publishing.

3. Office for National Statistics (2004) 'News Release: One in ten children has a mental disorder.' Available at http://webarchive.nationalarchives. gov.uk/20140721132900/www.statistics.gov.uk/ pdfdir/cmd0805.pdf, accessed on 3 December 2015.

4. Synergy Healthcare Research: 'ADHD in the UK Today.' Survey of 50 child and adolescent psychiatrists and 75 paediatricians, July 2003.

5. ADDISS Families Survey 2006.

6. Young, S.J., Adamou, M., Bolea, B., Gudjonsson, G. *et al.* (2011) 'The identification and management of ADHD offenders within the criminal justice system: a consensus statement from the UK Adult ADHD Network and criminal justice agencies.' *BMC Psychiatry*.

7. American Psychiatric Association (2013) *Diagnostic and Statistical Manual of Mental Disorders, 5th edition*. Arlington, VA: APA.

8. World Health Organization (1993) *The ICD-10 Classification of Mental and Behavioural Disorders: Diagnostic Criteria for Research*. Geneva: WHO.

About the Author

Originally a Londoner, Alison Thompson has spent much of the last 21 years as a single parent bringing up her children in urban Hampshire and rural Oxfordshire. Having worked in a variety of part-time jobs while the children were small, she graduated with a first-class honours degree in Media Technology and Production as a mature student, worked as a picture research manager for the world's third largest stock photography library, and then set up her own business.

Nowadays Alison runs two businesses from her home in rural Oxfordshire. As The Proof Fairy, she helps aspiring authors to write and self-publish books; meanwhile, her interest in ADHD led her to train as a coach and she now offers support and advice to parents under the banner of ADHD Kids.

Alison loves helping people and outside the office she is a volunteer for an ADHD support group and a local refugee charity. In the odd spare moment she enjoys photography, reading, motorsports, football, art journalling and swimming, and she is on a lifetime mission to learn the guitar and knit a scarf.

Alison was shortlisted for the mother@work Most Exceptional Working Mother award in 2008 and attended the final at 11 Downing Street. She was also a semi-finalist in the Venus Awards Oxfordshire 2014 in both the Business Mother and Inspirational Woman categories.

The Boy from Hell: Life with a Child with ADHD is her first book but is not likely to be her last!

To contact Alison:

Email: alison@adhdkids.org.uk

Twitter: @proof_fairy or @ADHD_Kids

You can find out more about this book and ADHD in general at www.adhdkids.org.uk.

Find out about her day job at www.theprooffairy. com.

If you have any suggestions, recommendations, tips or techniques that you'd like to pass on, please email alison@adhdkids.org.uk and they will be considered for inclusion in the next edition.